Making Schools *Work*

For *parents* of school-age children

by

Robert F. Mager

Bob Mager

Mager Associates, Inc.
Carefree, AZ

Making Schools *Work*

Cover page design by Tony Amato, amato image Design, Inc. Layout design and technical editing by Eileen Mager.

Printed in the United States of America
ISBN: 9781622091553

Non-Fiction Books by Robert F. Mager ...

Preparing Instructional Objectives, Revised Third Edition

Measuring Instructional Results, Revised Third Edition

Analyzing Performance Problems, Revised Third Edition (with Peter Pipe)

Goal Analysis, Revised Third Edition

How to Turn Learners On . . . without turning them off, Revised Third Edition

Making Instruction Work, Revised Third Edition

What Every Manager Should Know About Training, Second Edition

Troubleshooting the Troubleshooting Course

Life in the Pinball Machine, Second Edition

Contents

What's This About?

Have you ever wondered *exactly* what goes on in so many public schools that keeps them from succeeding? Is it *really*, according to the persistent propaganda, a lack of money? Or is it a shortage of skilled teachers? Could it be that the students themselves are incapable of learning? Or that the government deliberately prevents schools from modernizing their practices? Or something else entirely?

School officials tell us their mission is to send students away with the life skills they need to survive and prosper in the world at large. That's admirable. Yet kids continue to graduate from high school still unable to:

- read and understand such things as the content of a newspaper, an instruction manual, or an apartment lease (it doesn't take twelve years *not* to teach kids to read, write, and count);
- do simple math;
- speak our language clearly;
- discuss aspects of this country's history, and describe basic tenets of our Constitution.

Also, consider that many high school graduates are so unprepared for college-level work they must be provided with remedial coursework in English, math, and more. But why should colleges—and industry—be saddled with the job of making up for what public schools should be doing, but aren't? *Exactly* what is causing those schools to continually miss the mark??

To find out, follow Ricky Dinker, a bright ten-year-old fifth-grader, as he explains to his Dad why he wants to buy his own school. Why? "Because," Ricky says, "I'm living in it every day and see the dorky things they do that keep them from succeeding." He then describes how he would eliminate some of the glaring obstacles strewn along the path to excellence. He tells us how to dissolve the so-called "motivation" problem, how to decrease the "dropout" rate, and guarantee student success at what is being taught, all without increasing the homework load or lengthening the school day. And that's just for starters.

So step into Ricky's world as he and his Dad discuss his plans for fixing "his" school so it produces students who can, in fact, do what they are expected to be able to do. Along the way, you'll discover ways to dissolve some of the obstacles and barricades to success in your *own* children's school environment.

It's worth a try ... especially since all of Ricky's solutions have been proven to work, and almost all of them are free.

Robert F. Mager
Carefree, Arizona

Scene 1

The Slippery Grading Slope

Ricky Dinker picked up his very own straight-backed chair and carried it to the yard. His parents had bought it at a neighborhood flea market for three whole dollars and presented it to him for his tenth birthday. He fell in love with it as soon as he saw the wicker seat with the spaceship hand-painted on its back. It wasn't that it was particularly comfortable, but it was *his* chair, and just *his* size.

Without speaking, Ricky placed the chair next to the hammock where his father lounged each afternoon after returning from work. He sat quietly until his Dad finished reading the newspaper, having learned this approach would put his father in a better mood for a man-to-man talk.

When at last the paper was folded and dropped to the cool grass beneath him, Dad looked up and said, "I see you've brought your chair. That means we need to have a talk, right?"

"Yes, sir," Ricky said.

"Is this about your allowance?"

"No, sir. It's about school."

"I see. You're flunking all your courses and they're about to throw you out on your butt?"

"Good one, Dad." Ricky knew his father was joking; it was no secret he was what the school people referred to as a "gifted student." It was unthinkable he could fail any of the courses he was forced to endure—most of which he referred to as "trivial pursuits." He also knew the teachers called him "that pain-in-the-ass kid" behind his back, a label he wore with pride.

"Well, Dad, they're mad at me for dozing off in class. But no, I'm not failing anything."

"Then what? Trouble with a bully? Girlfriend pushing for a lifetime commitment?"

"Nothin' like that, Dad. I want to talk about a loan."

"So it's about money?"

"In a way," Ricky said, crossing one knee over the other like the big people did. "It's like this. If you can loan me a million dollars, I think I can buy the school."

"*Whoa.*" Ricky's father swung his legs over the edge of the hammock and hunkered down on the lawn facing his son. He knew better than to dismiss his offspring's wacky ideas out of hand—at the very least, they led to interesting discussions. "May I ask *why* you want to buy the school?"

"They're doing some pretty dorky things, Dad. If I owned it, I could make it work a lot better."

"And why do you think you could make it work

better?"

"Because I'm living in it. I'm in the middle of the hokey things they do, so I get to see things nobody else seems to pay much attention to. I get to *feel* the effects of the things that are ... uh, out of whack."

"And what makes you think they're out of whack?"

"Well," Ricky said, "when I started noticing some weird things going on, I got to thinking about why the schools exist in the first place. That's when I began to notice some things the schools are doing that just don't match up with what they say they're *supposed* to be doing."

"Uh huh," Dad said. "And what do they say they're supposed to be doing?"

"Well, they say they're supposed to give kids the skills and tools they'll need in the real world ... you know, to turn them into 'well-rounded adults.' They use other fuzzy words to say what the schools are supposed to be doing, but that's about it."

"But—?" Dad prompted.

"But then, they throw all kinds of rocks in the road that keep that from happening."

"Rocks?"

"Obstacles. You know, things that get in the way of getting the results the schools say they want."

"Got an example of one of these obstacles?"

"Sure. For one thing, the grading system stinks."

Oh-oh, this is going to be serious business, his

father thought. *I'd better get my brain in gear.* It was hard enough keeping up with a super-bright ten-year-old kid when they talked about familiar subjects, like sports. When it looked like the discussion might sail over his head, Dad needed to focus his full attention. "You say you're not flunking anything, but the grading system stinks?" Dad ventured. "What brought that on?"

"Yeah, like it doesn't make sense. I didn't think anything about it until they jerked me out of my math class and stuck me into another one."

"You don't like the teacher?"

"Nuthin' like that, Dad. When you were in school, did they grade on the letter system? You know, 'A's and 'B's, and such?"

"Sure. The smart kids got 'A's and the dumb ones got 'D's and 'F's. That what you mean?"

"Yeah. Well, for a long time, I thought those grades were supposed to show how well you learned the subject."

"But now you don't believe that?"

"Not any more. Those grades don't say *anything* about how well *I* learned the subject. They only say something about where I stand next to other kids in my class."

"Can you say that in words even a Dad can understand?"

"Well, it won't be easy, but I'll try." Ricky added a mischievous grin to the comment.

"Ouch."

"Okay, here goes. There's lots of stuff wrong with the grading system, but let's start with an easy one. Suppose you were a 'B' student in your Brownie class and they moved you to the Greenie class where all the kids happened to be smarter. All of a sudden you could be a 'D' student."

"Really? *Why?*"

"Because you wouldn't compare as well against the Greenies as you did against the Brownies. You would be the *same* kid doing the *same* kind of work, but your grade would be lower because they used a different grading yardstick. Same work—different grade. That stinks, don't you think?"

"Sure sounds like it. Let me see if I've got this straight. You're saying they compare *your* work with the work of the *other* kids and base the final grade on that. Right?"

"Yeah. It's called 'grading on the curve.' You know what that is, don't you?"

"Uh ... after a lifetime struggling through the public school system, I think I've got the hang of it." Dad smiled at Ricky's attempt to school him in the basics.

"What I don't get is why *my* grade should be based on how well *other* kids do. If a grade is supposed to say something about how well *I've* learned what I was supposed to learn, then it ought to be based on the quality of *my* work— regardless of how other kids perform, don't you think?"

"Makes sense to me," Dad said.

"So now, if I'm sitting in a classroom with a different bunch of students, but I'm doing the same work I did in the first classroom, and if the school is *truly* grading me on the quality of my work, my grade shouldn't change. It shouldn't matter how great or lousy I look in comparison with the other students."

"Good point," Dad said, stroking his chin. "If the teachers want to know if you've learned to hit a target, they should ask you to shoot at the target and then count the number of times you hit it."

"Right on. They should compare my work to what *I'm* supposed to be learning to do."

"So," Dad continued, "if you only hit the target half the time, you'd have a score of fifty percent. Then, if the instructor had to turn that number into a grade, he might call that fifty-percent performance a 'C.'"

"You got it, Pops."

"But that grade shouldn't have anything to do with what the other students did—it should remain a 'C' *regardless* of how well or poorly the other students performed."

"Very good, Dad. I think you've got it." Ricky reached over and playfully patted his father's head. "And if I went to another shooting range with another instructor, and only hit bulls-eyes half the time, I'd *still* be fifty percent successful, even if all the other students *never* hit the target—or even if they hit bulls-eyes all the time."

"That's true," Dad said.

"Right. My grade would be based on what *I* accomplished, and that wouldn't change no matter *what* the other students did."

"I think I get it," Dad said.

"But the school's way of doing things is even shiftier than just basing grades on the average performance of the class."

"Oh? How so?"

"Sometimes they just change the grading yardstick."

"Yardstick?"

"The rules, Dad, they just change the rules. Even if the teachers are given the same kind of yardstick—grading rules—in both classes, those yardsticks can change—even within a single class."

"How can that be?"

"Okay, here it is. Let's say Joe and Mary both get all the answers right on a spelling test. They should both get 'A's, right?"

"Of course. If they both accomplish as expected, they both deserve an 'A.'"

"But suppose the teacher gives Mary an 'A,' and Joe a 'B.' What would you think about that?"

"That would be unfair. But how could that happen?"

"Well, the teacher tells Joe, 'You spelled all the words right, but your messy paper was handed in late and was hard to read, so I'm going to have to take ten points off.' Or, 'You used pencil instead of ink, so I'm going to have to take another ten points off.' Kinda like telling Joe she's adding a few inches to his yardstick. See?"

"You're saying the smudginess, or pencil color, doesn't have anything to do with revealing how well Joe did at spelling, but his grade might be based in part on those irrelevant things *anyhow?*"

"Right. It's like the yardsticks are made of rubber. Sometimes they take points off for chewing gum in class, or because you were a little late, or because of all sorts of other reasons. I dunno. Maybe they do that to help them spread kids out on their curve. Maybe they think it's *okay* to do that sort of thing. Whatever the reason, you never know when they're going to change the rules of the game."

"Boy," Dad said, "I couldn't get away with that at the Police Academy."

"'Course not. *Your* guys are teaching things to cop cadets who will have to *prove* they've actually learned, even if it takes one guy longer to learn it than another guy. If you want to find out if they can shoot, you score their shooting success. You couldn't get away with fudging a student's grade just because his butt crack was showing."

"Good one," Dad chuckled. "Y'know, I remember all those loosey-goosey grading practices. It's one of the reasons I quit teaching high school after only three years. I wanted to work where it mattered whether the students learned or not, someplace where there were consequences for learning or not learning. That's mainly why I signed up as a Training Supervisor at the Police Academy. There, if we want to know how well the student accomplished the goals of the lessons—and of course, we do—we look at how well he or she performed at the end of the learning period."

"Sure. Anything else would be irrelevant. But

if your students happened to learn useful skills from other places—skills that were relevant to what you were teaching them—you'd think that was fine, right?"

"Of course," Dad said. "But what are you getting at?"

"Just that, fortunately for me, school isn't the *only* place I can, and do, learn stuff."

"Oh? Where else do you learn?"

"Pretty much anywhere," Ricky replied. "For example, the library and the web are great sources of information. Y'know, I think I learn more from places *outside* the school than I do *in* it. Come to think of it, I think *most* people learn from sources outside the schools."

"Hmm," Dad said. "Why do you suppose that is?"

"Lots of reasons. For one thing, the teachers are too occupied with busywork—you know, things that don't have anything to do with teaching, like paperwork—to spend much time actually teaching."

"I can't argue with that," Dad said. "Teachers have been loaded down with tasks better suited for babysitters and bookkeepers for as long as I can remember."

"Right on," Ricky said. "It's kinda like making a surgeon clean up the operating room after he's done all his operating, or like making a manager answer his own phones and do all the typing and filing stuff. It's a wonder teachers have any time left at all to focus on teaching."

"You've got it," Dad said.

"Sometimes," Ricky said, "I think that kind of sloppiness is built into the system on purpose. You know, if you keep the teachers too busy with scutwork to give them much time to actually teach, it's easier to keep the kids dumbed down and easier to control."

"Whoa," Dad said. "You really *have* been peeking under the academic tent."

"Yeah, a little. Besides, I spend a lot of time on the Homeschoolers website, and at the Khan Academy website. But we were talking about some of the specific dorky things the schools do."

"Right. Carry on."

"Okay, here's another example. An eighth-grader I know told me that, in his algebra class, the teacher does a pretty good job of teaching kids to solve simple math equations. She even gives them practice time during class. But when the final test time rolls around, she throws in some of those word problems. And he said they'd never even *seen* one of those, let alone learned how to *deal with* them."

"Ugh," Dad said. "I remember going through that when *I* was a kid. It's another example of teaching one thing and testing for something else."

"Right. Don't you need a different skill for solving those word problems than for solving problems with just numbers in them?"

"Yes, you do," Dad said. "So no matter how well you did with the word problems, it still didn't show how well you could solve *equations*. So how would you deal with that in *your* school?"

"I'd begin by making sure my teachers knew *why* they were teaching, and exactly *what* their students were expected to accomplish. Then I'd invent ways to make sure *both* the teachers *and* the students knew what the students should be able to do by the lesson's end."

"Sounds like a good start," Dad said. "That reminds me. One of my professors in a college course lectured to us by reading from the textbook. Then, on final test days he would slip in items asking about the *footnotes*. Can you believe that kind of skullduggery? That was really sneaky, because he *never even mentioned* footnotes during any of the classes. Once we learned his secret, though, we just studied the footnotes and skipped over most of the text."

"*Dinner!*" Mom called from the back porch. "Tonight we're having spiky balls with stinky juice."

"Oh boy, Dad—artichokes and garlic sauce. Race ya to the kitchen!"

Scene 2

De-Fuzzing Outcomes

On returning from work the following afternoon, Dad looked out the back window and saw his son already nestled by the hammock in his very own chair. *Hmm*, he thought, *Rick must be eager to continue our discussion from yesterday. I'd better pay close attention.*

"Hi, Rick. Have a good day in school?"

"Hi, Dad. Yeah, school was okay ... but I could make it better."

"So you've said. Notice I didn't bring my newspaper along today. I had a feeling you were chomping at the bit about something."

"Yes, sir. It's about what we were talking about when we got called to dinner."

"I remember," Dad said. "You told me that one could not find out how well students could perform unless one actually watched them *demonstrate* what they were supposed to have learned."

"Right," Ricky said. "Y'see, if the final assessment consists only of items asking for *approxima-*

tions of what the student is supposed to have learned, the teacher never finds out whether the student has actually achieved the objective of the lesson."

"Explain," Dad said.

"Okay. To use a simple task, suppose the student is supposed to learn how to tie his or her shoelaces. How would you find out whether the student accomplished that objective?"

"Well," Dad said, "Obviously, I'd ask to watch the student tie those laces."

"Of course," Ricky said. "But why not just ask the student to *describe* the process of shoelace-tying?"

"No," Dad said. "Asking for a *description* of the process may be useful *during* a course to assess progress, but it does NOT tell you whether the student can actually tie the laces. Describing is not the same as tying."

"Exactly," Ricky said. "You could also use multiple-choice items, I suppose, or a bunch of other types of items, but *none* of them would tell you whether the student could actually *do* the tying."

"I see it," Dad said. "Items asking only for *approximations* to accomplishment of the skill might be useful, but *only* for assessing *progress* toward achievement of the skill."

"Right on. That leads us to another part of the problem."

"Oh?"

"Yup," Ricky said. "When assessment items

ask *only* about what happened during the class sessions, that can be another example of bad practice."

"Why?" Dad asked. "What's wrong with testing students on what was taught in class?"

"Nothing—if what was taught in class matches what the objective calls for. But often, it doesn't. It might be only *part* of what the objective calls for. Or maybe the teacher spent the class time *talking about* it, rather than having the students actually *practice* it. In those cases, testing on what was taught in class won't tell the teacher whether—or how well—the students accomplished the actual *purpose of the lesson*."

"Well, of course, you're right," Dad said. "And it isn't fair to the student. When the class activities, like lectures and things, focus on what the *teacher* does, instead of on what the *student* is supposed to learn to do, the teacher might make up quizzes asking about what she did or said during class. If that happens, her final grade would not tell anyone how well the students had accomplished what they were supposed to learn; just what they remembered of what she did or said. In other words, the grade would deliver false information about the students' ability."

"But there's more," Ricky added. "Try this example. Suppose you're taking a cooking class and you've been told you would be learning how to bake a cake. And suppose the teacher spends the class time showing videos about how to bake cakes, and telling stories about the times she made mistakes while learning to bake, and shows pictures of her practice cakes that ended up in a pile of sludge. You get to see how the baking is done, and hear stories about mistakes to avoid, but when the end of the course comes around, you're faced with test items about what was on the videos and lectures."

Dad said, "So what is tested matches what was taught in class. But you're saying that in class I never got to actually practice *baking* a cake?"

"Right."

"Well, that would be a gigantic mismatch between the objective of the lesson and what was assessed, wouldn't it?"

"That's my point," Ricky said.

"So," Dad said, "how will you deal with that issue when you have your own school?"

"The main thing will be to make sure the kids are always clear about what they're supposed to be able to do, and make sure they have everything they need for accomplishing it. Another step will be to make sure *teachers* know what the students are expected to *accomplish*, so they'll know what their students should be practicing."

Dad nodded and said, "That makes sense. But if you let students in on the secret of what they're supposed to accomplish, they might be able to learn it by going to sources other than the class sessions. Right?"

"Sure. Like I mentioned yesterday, that's what some of us do. If the teacher isn't helping us learn what we're supposed to learn, we go to other sources to keep from flunking the course. Heck, with the web and all the other information at our fingertips, we can learn all sorts of stuff. Don't forget, *everybody* learns from sources other than schools and lectures. They can't help *not* doing it."

"You're right about that," Dad said. "As evidence, consider all the things kids learn outside of school that parents would rather they *not* learn."

"Good example," Ricky said. "That reminds me, one day I asked about something in a lesson we hadn't had yet, and the teacher frowned at me and said, 'Don't try to get ahead of the class.' I'm glad I didn't tell her I'd already read the whole textbook. Even so, it made me feel bad. It was a real downer."

"I can imagine," Dad said. "There seems to be no shortage of examples where teachers punish the very behavior they are trying to encourage—such as using homework as a form of punishment, as in 'Okay, just for that you can read *three* chapters of *Silas Marner* instead of just the one I originally assigned.' Got any other ways to eliminate the mismatches between the objectives, what was taught, and what was tested?"

"Uh-huh. When a teacher is creating lesson plans, I'll have a litttle checklist on which she can make notes about the important components of any lesson plan."

"Such as?" Dad prompted.

"You know ... the objective of the lesson, the content, the method of providing practice, and end-of-lesson assessment items. That way, she can make sure she's thought about all the key lesson components before fleshing out the lesson plan."

"Good thinking," Dad said. "Got any other ideas about how to make sure each student gets a fair chance at learning what they're supposed to?"

"You bet. I'll use some of the successful teaching tactics already in existence. For one thing, I'll find ways to turn the classrom into a place where the students can work on reaching their goals individually, if they want. The teachers would be trained to be coaches—think consultants—ready to help individual students when they needed it."

"Sounds like a real challenge," Dad said.

"I know. I could never get a regular school to go for it—"

"Why not, if I may ask?"

"Because it would be too big a change from the status quo. For one thing, it would mean rearranging the classroom furniture. You know, instead of having the teacher standing in front of the room lecturing to a bunch of kids sitting in rows in front of her, there would be work tables for about two students each scattered around the room. That way, the teachers could move from one student to another to give individual attention—without bugging everybody else."

"I think I've got it," Dad said. "Your classroom would look a little more like a library study room."

"No, more like a card party. The tables would not be set up in rows."

"Right. Got it," Dad sad.

"Good. Okay if I change the subject a little?"

"Go for it."

"Okay," Ricky said, frowning. "It's those dog-gone multiple-choice questions. It seems that no matter what they're trying to teach me to do, they always use multiple-choice items to find out if I can do it. It's like the multiple-choice item is their holy grail of test items. You know— 'Hey there, need a test? Here's some multiple-choice items.' Whatever you want to know, no matter what's supposed to be assessed, they usually use multiple-choice items."

Dad said, "Why do you suppose that is?"

"Well, I guess it's because it's easier to score— at school they do it on a machine in a little room next to the principal's office. Many teachers actually think it's an 'objective' format just because they *can* machine-score it."

"Whether or not it will tell you what you want to know?"

"Yes, sir. For example, when you want to find out whether your cop cadets can fill out an accident report, do you give them a multiple-choice test?"

"Good grief, no. I set up an accident scene and give them a blank accident report form, then ask them to analyze the scene and fill out the report. That way, they'll be actually *doing* what they were supposed to learn to do."

Ricky pretended horror and held his hands to his head. "*What?* You don't use multiple-choice items? Or an essay test asking them to *describe* the procedure for making out the report?"

"Okay, okay, I get it," Dad said, laughing. "An assessment should be designed to find out how well the student has accomplished the purpose of the lesson. And to do that, the student's performance should be compared to the *objective* of the lesson, *not* to what was taught in the classroom, or on how well the other students performed. Right?"

"Absolutely."

"It seems obvious," Dad said. "But how would you deal with that in *your* school?"

"I'd do it just like you do at the Police Academy," Ricky said.

"Got an example?" Dad said.

"Well, in the case of a shooting course, everybody knows they'll have to learn to shoot because the testing will be done on the range. Right?"

"Sure."

"So it's pretty obvious to the students what they'll need to practice if they're ever gonna qualify."

"Uh-huh," Dad said.

"But in a regular school, the kids aren't always told what they're supposed to get good at—"

"Excuse me for interrupting, but what do you mean by 'they aren't told what they're supposed to get good at?'"

"Well," Ricky said, "everybody knows the *name* of the course they're taking and what it's *supposed* to be about, but they may not know *for sure* what they're expected to be able to *do* at the end of the course that they couldn't do before it started. And they don't know for sure whether the teacher will *actually* teach what the course name says it's about. That makes the kids have to try to guess what the final test will be about, even though they may know the results of those assessment items they were faced with along the way."

"How can teachers get away with something like that?" Dad asked.

"Easy. The big kids say their teachers get paid whether they teach anybody anything or not, and they don't get fired if they don't. It's like they don't have to be accountable for their work, so they can teach just about anything they want and nobody butts in. I think they call that 'academic freedom.' Uh ... I think it's more like 'a license to steal.'"

"Wait a minute. Don't they have to follow lesson plans?"

"Well, yeah, sort of," Ricky said. "I once took a peek at my teacher's plan—it was open on her desk—and I thought it was kind of vague. It said things like, 'Be able to appreciate' something, or 'Understand the importance of' something else. As a result of the fuzzy language often used to describe the teacher's goals, one teacher's course can actually be a lot different from another teacher's course with the same name."

"Makes you wonder how a thing like that can happen," Dad said.

"How do *you* think it happens?"

"If you ask me," Dad said, "I think it happens because each teacher has her own classroom and probably doesn't talk much about her lessons with the other teachers. Just as you said, it means one bunch of kids can learn different things from what another bunch learns, in the same course. Worse, neither bunch might learn what they actually need in order to prepare them for the next course coming down the pike. Or they might learn too much."

"Too much?"

"Well, I remember an incident that happened when I was teaching a seventh grade class. The teacher of Algebra II got all bent out of shape about the teacher of Algebra I—"

"How come?"

"Because the kids coming into his class from the Algebra I class already knew about half of what the Algebra II teacher was planning to teach. That was because the Algebra I teacher was using more effective teaching techniques than the Algebra II teacher was using. And, instead of the Algebra II teacher rejoicing over the fact his incoming students were already halfway through his Algebra II syllabus, he got angry. Can you imagine such a thing? Getting mad because the students already knew some things he was planning to teach them?"

"That's what I'm talking about," Ricky said.

"So how would *you* fix that kind of situation?" Dad said.

"Easy. I'd try to schedule things so students completing Algebra I would stay with the same teacher for Algebra II. That way, there wouldn't be a problem caused by the right hand not knowing what the left hand was doing."

"Good plan," Dad said. "Then what?"

"Well, whenever students began a new lesson, I'd make sure they knew exactly what they'd have to be able to do before they were allowed to move to the next lesson."

"Got it," Dad said. "There's another advantage to your plan."

"Oh?"

"If you can arrange things so students can learn at their own rates, they won't have to listen to lectures about the stuff they already know. And that would go a long way toward solving the re-dundancy problem."

"The *what* problem?

"The redundancy problem. There is a fair amount of repetition of the same material over the K-12 years," Dad said.

"Got an example?"

"Sure," Dad said. "How to use a simple micro-scope is taught in several different courses."

"Gotcha," Ricky replied. "There's something else I'd like to do. Suppose you're in an English course and one of the things they want you to be able to do is spell a bunch of words. Right on the first day I'd give the kids a list of the words they'd be expected to learn to spell before I let them move to the next lesson. That way, they'd know exactly what to learn—and practice—to ace that spelling segment. They'd know where to focus their atten-tion and practice time."

"Sounds good," Dad said.

"Here's another example," Ricky continued.

"Suppose you're in a math course and you're supposed to learn how to solve certain kinds of problems. I'd make sure that before the students began each lesson they'd get to *see* samples of the kinds of problems they'll be expected to learn to solve. That way, they could focus their attention on the purpose of the lesson. They'd know what to practice, and how to tell when they've succeeded."

"Got it," Dad said. "You're saying it's not good enough simply to *tell* students what you're going to *talk about* during class sessions. Right? You would offer written descriptions giving kids a heads-up on what *they're* expected to be able to *do* before they can get checked off as having aced a lesson."

"Yes," Ricky said. "There's a big difference between teachers *telling* and students *doing*. I think my plan will help make sure the teachers stay focused on what needs to be *practiced* if their students are to have a chance at succeeding at learning the lesson."

"Still sounds good," Dad said. "Anything else?"

"Yeah. I'd also make sure that 'succeeding' means students will have to *demonstrate* the skills, not just show they can *talk about* doing them or answer multiple-guess questions about them. Y'see? Right off the bat, that solves two problems. It lets kids in on the secret of what they need to practice, and it pretty much washes out the need for grades."

"Wait a minute. How would it do that?"

"Well, if they've already shown they can *do* what's expected of them, why would you need to bother ginning up a letter grade? If they're as good at something as they're supposed to be—or maybe even better—they can be checked off on that lesson and be ready to move on. A grade wouldn't add any useful information."

"I'll have to think about that one," Dad said.

"Okay, let's go back to the pistol range," Ricky said. "What happens to you if your shooting score isn't as high as it's supposed to be?"

"Well, then I'm expected to keep practicing until my score comes up to where it should be," Dad replied.

"*What?*" It was Ricky's turn to pretend alarm. "They don't just *flunk* you if you don't measure up the *first* time?"

"What good would *that* do?" Dad said. "If the object of the game is for me to learn to shoot straight, then a flunking grade won't help. B*ut more practice would.*"

"Right on, Dad. If the kids are allowed to practice until they can *show* they've *mastered* the skill, who needs a grade that only shows them how well they compared with the other kids?"

"But if you let them practice until they've got it, some kids would master the lesson faster than others, wouldn't they?"

"Of course they would," Ricky said. "Not everyone learns at the same rate, Dad. I've learned on the homeschooling websites that most homeschoolers don't even know what 'grade' they're in.

Because each student gets to learn at his, or her, own rate, one student might be working at a first grade level while his neighbor is working at the third grade level, or even fourth or fifth grade level. And so on."

"I see that," Dad said.

"So, Dad, let me ask you this: Why does a course have to end on the same day for everybody? What's so magical about *that*? I think making a course the same length for everybody is mainly a convenience for teachers and administrators, and maybe to make some state law happy. It doesn't have anything to do with making learning more efficient for the students."

"I see that, too," Dad said, "but if they all got to practice until they mastered the skills, wouldn't they all have to be given 'A's?"

"What's wrong with that?" Ricky replied. "Aren't the schools *supposed* to be about making learning happen, instead of just finding ways to spread kids out on some make-believe curve? Try this on for size: Suppose we worked in a refrigerator factory and our team had to make a working refrigerator within a given time limit. And suppose our fridge was only two-thirds finished when the time limit was up. What should happen?"

"Well, they should let us keep on working until the job was done, right?"

"Of course," Ricky said. "But if the *school* was running the factory they just might give you a grade based on how much you accomplished within the time limit, and then send your product out to be sold."

"Now you're being silly," Dad said. "Nobody would send products out into the world if they *knew* they were defective, would they?"

"Oh, *yeah*? Then how come we send so many graduates, who can barely read or write, out into the world with diplomas?"

"Touché." Dad enjoyed pretending ignorance to help his son think through the tricky issues. It made him smile.

"*Dinner!*" Mom called from the back porch.

"Oh-oh," Dad said. "We'd better hustle, or Mom might make us eat zucchini again ... and no dessert."

"Oh, no! Anything but *that*," Ricky shouted, racing his Dad toward the house.

Scene 3

Multiple Bosses Don't Fly

As was his custom, Ricky Dinker waited patiently for his Dad to finish reading his evening paper.

"I see it's time for another man-to-man talk," Dad said, letting his newspaper slide to the ground.

"Yes, sir, if you have the time."

"What is it this time?" his father asked. "They won't let you sign up for basket-weaving? Too many girls hitting on you?"

Ricky knew his father was joking, so replied in kind. "No, they won't let me have any scalpels for my girl-dissecting experiments."

"You want to disassemble girls? What the heck for?"

"To find out how they work. I haven't been able to figure out what makes them tick. I thought if I took one apart I could find out if there were any."

"Any what?"

"Principles of operation."

"Uh-huh." His father wanted to tell him he'd hit upon one of the world's oldest mysteries, but decided to hold his tongue.

"But I think I'd have trouble putting them back together again," Ricky continued. "I know where some of the parts go, but until I learn how they work, I think I'd mess it up."

"Why don't you just take apart a nuclear reactor? That would be a lot easier."

"Mebbe so, but not as useful in the real world."

"Okay, you win," Dad conceded. "So what is it you want to talk about?"

"Actually, it's about school again."

"I see. You still want a million dollars to buy the school?"

"Yes, sir. Like I've been telling you, there's a bunch of ways I could make it work better. But there's something I think you could help me sort out."

"That's a switch. How can I help?"

"Well, how many bosses do you report to?"

"Come again?"

"How many people get to tell you what to do?"

"Why, just one, of course. I report to my boss, he reports to his, and so on up the ladder."

"I thought so," Ricky said. "What would happen if you had *four* or *five* different bosses to report to—all at the same time?"

Dad snorted. "Ha. *Chaos* would happen. It wouldn't work. They'd all be pressuring me to complete *their* assignments with little regard for what the other bosses wanted me to do. Why do you ask?"

"That's the way the school works. The kids in the higher grades have as many bosses as they have teachers."

Dad scratched his chin. "Y'know, I never thought about it that way."

"It's true. In the upper grades, each subject is taught by a different teacher. They don't seem to talk much with one another about things like homework assignments, so each teacher hums along like she's the only one making demands on the kids' time."

"What about in the fifth grade where you are?"

"We only have one or two teachers, so the homework problem isn't so bad. But in the upper grades, having several teachers at the same time means some take up more than their fair share of homework time. And the big kids tell me it doesn't work."

"*How* doesn't it work?" Dad rolled off the hammock and sat on the grass in front of his son, now completely intrigued by the conversation.

"Okay," Ricky said, warming to his subject. "Suppose there's an English assessment—you know, test—tomorrow. Tonight you're likely to spend all your study time cramming for that sub-ject, and ignore the *other* homework assignments, right?"

"Probably," Dad said. "Not a good idea, though. What you learn through cramming often doesn't stick as well as a more balanced, spaced-practice approach."

"Uh-huh. And teachers who give one or more assessments during each week sop up even more study time."

"Is that bad?"

"Sure is. Because you're forced to spend most of your time trying to satisfy the squeakiest of the homework wheels—you know, the homework gluttons."

"Yes, I see that," Dad said. "That's one of the reasons the concept of multiple bosses doesn't work."

"There's another crazy thing about it, too."

"Oh?"

"Yeah," Ricky said. "Suppose the squeakiest wheel is the teacher who does one of the courses in English lit, for example."

"Okay, I'm supposing."

"And suppose she loads you down with reading assignments that'll take up all—or more—of your study time. Then, she gives a weekly assessment, and on top of that she tells you that *half* your *final* grade will be based on those weekly tests."

"So?" Dad prodded.

"So that means half your final grade will be based on how you did *while you were still learning,* instead of on how well you did at the end of the learning time. That's kinda like finally learning how to shoot baskets every time you try, then having half your grade based on the number the times you missed the hoop while you were learning. What do you think about that?"

"Using your kind of language," Dad said, "I'd say it stinks. A final grade should be based on your final level of accomplishment, not on the mistakes you made while learning and practicing."

"Yes," Ricky said. "What the heck is school for, anyhow? If it's to teach us subjects and how to solve problems and stuff, and if we end up learning it, why should they count the mistakes we made along the way? If the goal of the school is to grow the skills and knowledge of its students, you would think it would be obvious to them that this is a dumb practice."

"Remind me again what practice we're talking about."

"The practice of including weekly assessment results when counting up the final grade."

"Right," Dad said. "That would be like grading a music student's ability to play the trombone by adding up the number of sour notes he honked while practicing."

"Yup. To make it worse," Ricky said, "if the one hogging the most homework time happens to be teaching the least important subject—least important to your personal growth—that means that not only is she wasting your time, she's wasting *more* of your time than if she *didn't* base part of your final grade on the quizzes she gave while you were still learning the subject."

Dad scrunched up his forehead and prompted, "Can you give me an example?"

"Sure thing. Suppose you were taking a course

in basket-weaving and the teacher gave weekly quizzes. Then she graded you on the basis of how many mistakes you made on those quizzes. Then, she added the score you made on the final exam to the average score you made on the weekly quizzes. In this example, suppose you made a perfect score on the final exam—which should earn you an 'A.'"

"Makes sense," Dad said.

"But suppose you made some mistakes on the weekly quizzes, earning you an average 'C' or less. If the scores on the quizzes were used as half your final grade, you'd be getting a grade, at least half of which was based on no-longer-relevant data."

"I can see that," Dad said. "At the very least, your grade would not reflect your achievement. But do you think that's a realistic example?"

"Sure is."

"So how would you fix that in *your* school?"

"Well, first off, I'd make each teacher show the students, in writing, her rules for grading. Then I'd post them on the bulletin board. Once the other teachers found out who's sopping up all the study time, they'd probably revolt and lock the homework glutton in my pillory."

"Uh-huh," Dad said, trying hard not to laugh. "You'll have a pillory in your school?"

"Of course. Hey, we already got one in my regular school."

Dad's eyebrows flew skyward. "You *do?*"

"Yeah. It's called the Principal's Office. A trip to the PO can be about as much fun as sticking your head in a pillory, don'cha know." Ricky laughed at his own joke.

"Okay, I get it," Dad said. "So the first thing you'd do is publicize the grading rules used by each teacher. Good thinking. But what else would you do to solve the lopsided homework assignment problem?"

"Well, that's a little complicated to explain, but I'll try."

"Thanks a bunch," Dad said, smirking.

"Okay, it's like this. As it is now, students work on one subject until the bell rings, then rush down the hall for a shot of a different subject, taught by a different teacher."

"That's in the upper grades, right?"

"Mostly, yeah."

"So what's wrong with that? That's the way it's been done since Noah forgot to collect dinosaurs for his ark."

"Good one, Dad. But don't you see? That system is one of the rocks in the students' learning path."

"It is? How?"

"That bell arbitrarily makes the kids turn their heads off of one subject, then turn it on to another subject, *ready or not.*"

"So?"

"That's not so bad by itself, but the bell might ring at just the *wrong* time for the *student.*"

"How?"

"Try this. Suppose your cadets on the firing line are expected to shoot a string of ten practice shots, and right in the middle of doing that, a bell rings and they have to stop."

"I get it," Dad said. "That would be dumb, not to mention frustrating. So how would you handle it?"

Warming to his subject, Ricky said, "Okay, here it is. Pretend you're *really* more interested in the kids' learning than in just going along with a bunch of arbitrary rules."

"Okay, I'm pretending."

"Now pretend you're in a school where each schoolroom is used for a single subject. For example, the chemistry lab is at one end of the hall and has all the equipment and books needed for that course. Next door is an English room that has all the books and things needed to teach that subject."

"Okay, I can see that."

"Now imagine you have a kind of road map that shows you the entire course at a glance."

"How does it do that?" Dad asked.

"Here's a simple example of what a map might look like. Each bubble represents a task or skill to be learned, and the arrows tell the student which bubbles have to be learned before another one can be attacked."

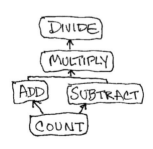

"Uh-huh. How do you read it?" Dad asked.

"You start from the bottom and work your way up. For example, on this little map fragment, you would be expected to learn to count to one hundred before you could learn to add or subtract single and double-digit numbers."

"Makes sense," Dad said.

"But it also shows that it's *your* choice whether you learn to add or subtract first. See? There's no arrow connecting the 'add' and 'subtract' bubbles. The map *also* shows you need to learn to add *and* subtract before you tried multiplication. And you'd have to learn multiplication before you moved to division."

"I see," Dad said. "And you're saying the map could show all the tasks and skills you would be expected to learn during the entire course?"

"Yes. Here's an example of what a complete course map might look like. You don't need to know what skills the bubbles represent—just notice how easy it would be to figure out how to work your way through the course if you were allowed to do so."

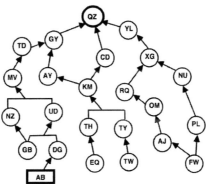

"I see that. But how would I know what the symbols inside the bubbles meant?"

"You'd have a list of course objectives on the page following the map—all you'd have to do is check it."

"You know," Dad said, "I think you've got something the students would really like. It lets them in on the secret of what the course is really about."

"Not only that, Dad. The map is a tool for giving kids as much freedom to drive their own learning as the subject matter will allow. And I'm told the kids get a lot of satisfaction from getting the bubbles signed off; they can actually *see* the progress they're making as they learn. Besides that, because this pretend school doesn't have a bell, it lets students stay with one subject as long as they want before tackling another one. And the kids can look at their map any time to see how all the lessons are connected."

"Sounds good. But how do the kids know when to move from one room to the next?"

"Simple. When a kid thinks he has aced the objective of one of the lessons, he'll signal a teacher and ask her to watch him prove he's ready to move on. Or, he might just be tired of working on *this* lesson—so he'll just glance at his map to see which other subjects he's qualified to work on on."

"I like it. That would mean the teacher would function more like a coach ready to help anyone who needed it, and could do it without disrupting an entire class."

"Yup. And that's a toenail summary of how I would change my school from being controlled by the clock and the bell, to one controlled by the progress of the student."

Dad drummed his fingers on a knee while digesting what he had just heard. "Sounds good, but it's pretty radical, you know."

"I know it. That's why I need the million bucks to buy my own school. They'd *never* let me try this in a regular school."

"You got *that* right. But wait a minute. Come to think of it, something like what you're describing has already been tried in the past. Would you like to hear about one instance?"

"You bet," Ricky said.

"Okay, Dad began, "this happened in the Duluth school system way back during the nineteen-sixties, when dinosaurs were still pooping up the landscape."

"You sure paint a vivid image."

"Well, I try," Dad said, with a grin. "Anyhow, the assistant superintendent, a Dr. Tory Esbensen, got the okay to try a version of the system you just described. First, he installed the system in grades five and six, then each year added another grade in each direction."

"Huh?"

"For the first year, the program was installed in grades five and six, then in the second year, he added grades four and seven to the system, and so on."

"Got it. So how did it work out?"

"Pretty well. The kids loved it and worked their tails off to finish projects, then demonstrate to the teacher they could do what the lesson called for. The kids got real kicks from getting a unit signed off. They treated it like an immediate reward for a real accomplishment, which it really was. Better yet, the kids got so involved with learning, they often didn't want to leave at the end of the school day. I tell you, there was no problem with motivation in *that* school."

"Sounds really good," Ricky said.

"But when the system got added to the tenth grade, things got a little dicey."

"Why?"

"Well," Dad continued, "the high school building had three floors, y'see. They put the seniors on the ground floor, the juniors on the middle floor, and the freshmen on the top floor, because they were the newbies. But when those newbies caught on that they were free to move around, they took tables and chairs from the classrooms and slopped out into the hallway to study. That gave them more room to work, and they could work together—or by themselves—without bothering anybody else."

"Sounds like it worked like gang-busters."

"It did, indeed," Dad said. "But when the senior kids on the first floor found out the *freshmen* on the third floor could move around at will, and *they* couldn't, they groused about it, big time. Remember, the system hadn't yet been installed in the eleventh and twelfth grades. So that was a problem."

Ricky nodded. "I can see that happening, but I think I could fix that. Any other downsides?"

"Oh, yes," Dad said. "The kids in the Elementary grades, who were already on the system, really ticked off the Fire Commissioner when they rolled their butcher paper along the hallway to paint murals on. Worse, they began sticking paper flowers onto the fire extinguishers hanging in the halls. The kids were just exercising their creativity, of course, but it drove the fire guys bonkers. It was like creativity wasn't allowed. Finally, the fire guys had to shut it down because it was illegal to clutter the hallways and cover up the fire equipment with paper flowers and stuff."

"Aww."

"One other thing," Dad continued. "Like I said, lots of the kids didn't want to go home when the school day ended, because they wanted to finish a project they were working on. That meant one or two teachers had to hang around after school, to monitor the kids. That ticked the teachers off."

Glued to his Dad's anecdote, Ricky asked, "So how did it all work out?"

"Well," Dad said, "when the super who initiated the project left for a job in another state, the whole system was soon cancelled. I guess the establishment just couldn't stand that much academic success."

"You just made that whole thing up, didn't you?" Ricky said.

"No, sir. It's the honest truth. And I've read about other projects like that one, too. So yes, the basics of your system were tried even before *I* was born."

"Are any of them still working?"

"Oh, yes," Dad said, "but I don't know of any examples in the public school systems. The successful examples I know about are all in organizations *other* than the public schools."

"Bummer. How come not in the public school system?"

"I think you already know the answer to that," Dad said. "Why is it you want your own school?"

"Got it," Ricky said. "The schools are failing because they insist on using outdated teaching techniques."

"Even so, there *is* a relatively ancient example of something like the system we're talking about."

"Oh? What?"

"Remember the one-room schoolhouses of the early days?"

Chuckling, Ricky said, "You mean back when you were a little kid and fire hadn't yet been invented? No, can't say as I do."

"Smarty. Well, back then, they had these one-room schoolhouses, so the kids of all the 'grades' had to gather in the same room at the same time. The teacher couldn't just lecture, you see, because the kids were spread out over all the grades."

"Gee," Ricky said, "that would be tough to manage."

"You bet. Well, the teacher assigned each kid

a project at their individual level. They moved ahead as fast—or slowly—as their talent allowed. There was no bell to interrupt the flow of learning. The teacher moved around the room and helped as many kids as she could with the time she had. Your system sounds something like that, but more modern and efficient."

"Thanks for the whoop. Don't you guys do something like that at the Police Academy?"

"We try. We hold the lectures to a minimum and schedule at least half of each class period for actual practice of what's being learned. Gives cadets a better chance at remembering new material. But your way would be even better."

Ricky had a sudden thought and scrunched his face in puzzlement. "But what happens if one of your cadets learns the stuff a lot quicker than the others do? That must happen to you a lot."

"All the time."

"So do you let your cadets go outside and play, or go home, until the next course starts?"

"You're kidding, right?" Dad smiled at the image of a bunch of cops-to-be playing in sandboxes outside the training building. "Well, in a way, yes. When our cadets can demonstrate they've learned what they're supposed to learn before the time segment is up, they're given a list of suggestions about what they might do until their next segment begins."

"Things like what?"

"Most of the time, they prefer to spend extra time practicing their marksmanship, or working out in the gym, or getting coached on what they're having trouble understanding."

"Well, in *my* school," Ricky said, "kids who finish a project before the day is over will be free to begin another lesson, or quit for the day.   Uh … wait. Stop the train. I'll have to think about the quitting for the day thing. If kids can quit early and are allowed to go home, the parents will freak out, big time. They don't want their kids showing up before the official day ends. They might show up when their parents were still at work—not good for little kids. Besides, it would also drive the bus drivers bonkers. They live by the clock, you know. Anyhow, students will still move ahead at their own pace."

"Whoa, there. If you did that, you might not have much need for homework."

Ricky beamed. "Yeah, imagine that! My school would do away with most of it."

"Oh? How?"

"Well, since I'll arrange things so the kids can spend more time studying and practicing *during the school day*—instead of listening to lectures and doing busywork—they'll already have finished most of what used to be homework before the day ends. 'Course, some things have to be practiced more than others, like speaking another language, or speaking clearly, or learning to play a musical instrument."

"Right on," Dad said. "A lot of homework exists mostly because teachers have to spend a lot of time doing non-teaching tasks—like paperwork.

They have a big load of busywork tasks thrown at them that waste time that could be used for teaching. But that can easily be cured by giving teachers an assistant to handle most of it."

"*Dinner*, boys," Ricky heard his mother call from the back porch. "We're having your favorite tonight—squiggly worms and lumpy blood sauce."

Ricky leaped to his feet. "Oh, boy, Dad—spaghetti and meatballs!" Punching his Dad on the arm, he said, "Race you to the house! Don't forget to wash your hands."

Scene 4

Push-Outs

When Ricky saw his father's paper drop to the ground, he cleared his throat.

"Something stuck in your gullet?" Dad could tell it was time for another heart-to-heart talk, so he slid from the hammock and hunkered down beside his ten-year-old gifted son.

"No, sir. But if you've got a few minutes, I'd like to talk to you about school again."

"Uh-huh. You still after a loan of a million clams to buy the school?"

"Uh huh. But I've still got some glitches to work out on how I'll run it."

"Okay, what's on your mind?"

"It's like this, Dad. Suppose a restaurant refuses to set up a no-smoking section, and a couple of weeks later the manager notices that practically nobody goes there to eat anymore. What would you call those customers?"

Dad smirked and said, "Smart, I guess."

"You wouldn't call them *dropouts?*"

"Certainly not," Dad said. "It's the *restaurant's* problem if the customers choose to eat someplace else. If the owners decide to provide an eating environment that customers find yucky, they shouldn't be surprised if those people head for the hills."

"So what *should* the restaurant people do if they find their customers leaving for other eateries?" Ricky said.

"Well, they should try to find out what they're doing to drive the customers away."

Ricky pretended an expression of horror. "You mean the *restaurants* should try to find out what's pushing the people away?"

"Of course. For example, if you decided not to take baths anymore and began to stink, we might trade you in for another kid. At the very least, Mom and I might try standing as far from you as possible. If you didn't like that idea, you'd be wise to try to figure out what you're doing that's making us avoid you."

"You're saying it would be *my* fault if I stunk you to the other side of the street?"

"Absolutely," Dad said.

"But what if I got the city to pass a law that said you *had* to put up with my stinkiness?"

"That would be an insane way to go about it, don't you think?"

"I dunno. That's the way my school does it, you know—"

"Whoa. They *do?* Incredible. Tell me about it."

"Okay, it's like this. There are lots of reasons kids might decide to quit school—problems at home, or with the school, for instance—but as soon as the school people find out about kids who quit, they slap the 'dropout' label on them."

"So?"

"So by plastering the students with the 'dropout' label they can tell themselves that no matter *what* caused the student enough pain to leave school, it's the *student's* fault."

"I'm not sure I see the problem with that," Dad said.

"Try this," Ricky said. "Suppose you suddenly discovered that ninety percent of the cadets in Sergeant Yahoo's class haven't attended class for a week. They go to their other classes, but not to Yahoo's class. What would you do?"

Dad nodded. "I think I'm beginning to see the point. I'd try to find out what's going on in Yahoo's class that's driving them away."

"You wouldn't just call those guys 'dropouts' and move on to other things?"

"Of course not."

"Good," Ricky said. "Now suppose the cadets didn't just avoid Sergeant Yahoo's class; suppose they didn't show up at *any* classes?"

"In that case, I'd have to take a close look at the entire school, instead of just Yahoo. I'd have to find out if there's something *we're* doing that's causing cadets to leave. It could be any number of things, you know."

"Sure, it could," Ricky said. "That's the point.

But you'd try to find out what's going on in your school that's pushing the students away?"

"You bet I would."

"You wouldn't just call those guys 'dropouts' and be done with it?"

"Now you're being silly—wait a minute," Dad said. "Don't the schools send people out to discover why students drop out?"

"Sometimes. But mainly, I think they're more interested in dragging them back to school. They don't seem particularly interested in finding out *why* the student fled. After all, once they've labeled the student a 'dropout,' there's no reason to wonder what they might be doing to cause the out-dropping. So, even though they *might* take steps to find out why the student left school, the student is still the goat."

"Goat?"

"You know, the one to blame."

"I think I see," Dad said. "So what would you do in *your* school to fix the problem?"

"Well, first off, I'd make a policy that outlaws the 'dropout' word from the school vocabulary. I'd make everybody call them *push-outs*."

"And that would do what for you?"

"It would make it harder to knee-jerk and blame the student for leaving school. It would help put the focus on the *reasons* kids bug out. It would treat the out-dropping as a *symptom* of something in need of fixing. You said it yourself— there may be all sorts of reasons a kid drops out that have nothing to do with a kid's 'bad attitude.'

It may have something to do with the way the school is built, or how the teachers go about teaching, or boredom with the curriculum, or lack of parental support, or handicaps, or a whole bunch of other things. It may also be that the kid has bad eyesight and can't see well enough to get involved in the learning."

"I see that," Dad said. "You're suggesting there are many reasons a student may decide to leave school, and only some of those reasons can be blamed on the student."

"Uh-huh. My policy of ditching the 'dropout' label should also make it easier to get the administrators to wonder what may be going on in their school that's pushing kids away. Like I said, it isn't *always* what the teachers are doing that causes the push-out to skedaddle. Sometimes it's even the bullies, or a sick parent."

"Okay. And then what?"

"I'd create a 'Push-Out Index.' I'd use it as one clue about what I needed to do to lower that number."

"Explain," Dad said.

"Okay. If I found out that most push-outs were caused by something happening outside the school like, for example, parents who weren't interested, or able, to help their kids learn, I would focus on trying to make the parents aware of the results of their actions. But if I found out that some of the push-outs were caused by something to do with the school like, for example, the bullying, I'd focus on trying to solve that problem."

"I see what you're getting at," Dad said, "and it makes sense."

"You see, if the kids are bugging out because something about the school day is seriously punishing or boring, having them dragged back by the scruff of their necks isn't going to solve the problem."

"Explain."

"Eddie's sister—she's in college, learning to be a teacher—said schools get paid by how many kids are present, not by how well the teachers teach. It sounds nutty that schools are paid by the butt. But she says the more butts warming the chairs, the more money the school gets from the government, whether there's any learning going on in those butt-filled classrooms—or not. She says that in some states the schools get even *more* money if a butt is on medication. How's that for another example of rewarding undesirable behavior?"

"But—"

"Exactly!" Ricky said. "Don't forget that out-dropping is only a *symptom* of a problem. In my school, we'll work hard to find the cause of the bug-outery before we blame it all on the skedaddlers by calling them dropouts."

"Bug-outery?"

"I just made that up," Ricky said, displaying his silliest grin.

"But it isn't *always* the school's fault that students leave, is it?"

"That's what I've been telling you. It *isn't* always the school's fault. And it isn't always the

teachers' fault, either. But by calling kids dropouts, the kids might as well be wearing a sign
around their necks painted with with big red let-
ters saying 'IT'S ALL *MY* FAULT.'"

"Got an example?"

"Sure. Suppose the kid's home environment
doesn't believe in education, or suppose the parents ignore the kid's pleas for help. Or worse, suppose the parents make snotty remarks whenever
the kid tries to tell them what he learned in school
that day. What if other kids beat up on the kids
who try to learn, or call them names? There's lots
of reasons other than school policies and practices
that may be pushing the student out."

"I see that," Dad agreed.

"But at the same time, *some* of the reasons for
a kid bugging out should be plopped at the feet of
the schools—focusing hard on how they go about
doing things. But they don't seem to notice that
they are creating some of the things that are getting in the way of the learning."

"Such as?"

"The darn school bell, for example. We've
talked about this before. Lots of times the kids can
hardly wait for it to ring, you know, but sometimes
the teachers are having the kids doing such interesting projects, they want the period to last longer.
But it can't—because the bell *rules*. That can be
pretty frustrating, like someone swiping my lunch
before I'm finished eating it. It's a stumbling block
to learning."

"Uh-huh. What other obstacles do you see?"

"The instruction itself. Everybody talks about needing more money for the schools, but I've never heard *anybody* wonder about how their instructional *practices* might actually be getting in the way of the learning. For example, teachers should sing a happy song when students show interest in a subject, right?"

"Don't they?"

"Some do. But sometimes, when a kid gets so excited about knowing an answer and blurts it out, the teacher glares down at him and says, *'Don't-try-to-get-ahead-of-the-class!'* Can you guess how the kid feels? He's doing his best to show interest, and all he gets is slapped down for his trouble— and the teacher has flubbed another opportunity to say something positive to an eager student."

"But," Dad said, "you have to have some discipline, don't you?"

"Well, yeah, I guess, but it depends on what you mean by discipline. Even so, if the teacher wasn't lecturing while the students sat passively in their seats, the discipline thing couldn't even come up."

"It couldn't?"

"No," Ricky said. "If the teacher wasn't expecting everybody to sit quietly and pay attention to whatever she was saying, it wouldn't even be possible for kids to 'speak out of turn,' because there wouldn't be a 'turn' to speak out of."

"Explain, please?"

"I'll try. Suppose the classroom was run so that every student could work on their own project, either alone or in a small group. No lectures. Lots and lots of coaching, when it was needed, but no lectures. The kids would each be busy with whatever they were studying. In plain language, they couldn't interrupt something that didn't exist. Right?"

"Okay so far," Dad said.

"So if they were all busy with their own projects, they wouldn't be interrupting a lecture if they talked among themselves."

"Got it. If a shooter on my firing line wants help from an instructor, all he has to do is raise his hand—"

"Or fire off a couple of shots, maybe?" Ricky chuckled at his joke.

"Uh, right. But I see your point; there are all sorts of obstacles to learning, some perfectly obvious if only *somebody* would pay attention to them."

"Yeah," Ricky said. "Sometimes the textbooks are dry as a bone; other times the teacher doesn't know her subject well enough to teach it, so she just shows a lot of videos instead."

"Y'know," Dad said, "I've often wondered why you're still in fifth grade. How come you're not in college already?"

"Oh, no you *don't*," Ricky said, waggling a finger at his Dad. "They keep trying to get me to skip a couple of grades, but I always turn them down."

"May I ask why?"

"If I let them skip me a couple of grades, I'd be the smallest kid in the class, and the bullies would

pick on me. Also, I wouldn't know what the kids
learned during the grades I was skipped. I might
have missed something important and be kinda
lost until I could catch up."

"Is that all?"

"Not quite. My friend, Jimmy, he was skipped
over the fourth grade because he's a really smart
kid, and now he feels lost. Not only that, he feels
embarrassed because it makes him think he's not
as smart as he really is. So if you don't mind, I'll
just coast along with the gang I know. Y'see, I
know how to get along with kids my own age, and
with the teachers. And being smart is not a good
enough reason to force students to skip grades."

"Well, I'll be darned," Dad said. "I would never have guessed. How's Jimmy doing now?"

"Not bad. I'm helping him fill in the blanks. I
think I can get him up to snuff by the end of this
semester."

"That's really generous of you."

"Thanks. But Jimmy isn't the only kid I'm sort
of tutoring along. So I don't want to be skipped
and leave them behind."

"*Dinner,*" Mom called from the patio. "*Dead
squid pie for dessert tonight!*"

"Boy, I think I'll hire Mom to help run my
school. She sure knows how to lure people to her
table."

"Yeah," Dad conceded, "and we'd better scoot,
not to mention hurry up. Wouldn't want her to
think we're 'dinner dropouts.' Leave the chair."

Scene 5

Girls Are Different from Boys

Dad looked over the top of his newspaper at his son. "Hey, there, Rick. My nose tells me it's time for another man-to-man talk, right?"

Ricky crossed one leg over the other. "Yes, sir. It's about school again."

"What's the problem this time? Lost the key to the dungeon where you're planning to keep the girls?"

Being a brilliant ten-year-old, Ricky was up to the challenge. "Naw, I have a better idea. I'm gonna ditch the dungeon and put them into separate classes instead."

"What good would that do?"

"Well, they're a lot different from boys, you know—"

"Oh, you noticed?"

"C'mon, Dad, I'm not talking about the sex thing."

"Then what?"

"The learning thing. The way girls are made,

they can sit for hours, but boys have to move around a lot more. Since teachers are mostly made out of girls, boys are forced to learn in classrooms designed for girls."

"Oh? How so?"

"For one thing, if you can believe it, some of the classrooms still use those old desk-chairs made for right-handed people."

"True," Dad said, "but what does that have to do with making it hard for boys to pay attention?"

"It's painful to sit still in those hard chairs— and every other kind of chair they use—for long. Girls can do it better than boys, so that gives them an advantage right there."

"Do *all* the classrooms still use those old things?"

"Oh no, and that's a good thing. But it's just one example of how something about the school itself gets in the way of learning."

"Aha. What else interferes with learning?" Dad asked.

"The school bell. We talked about this before a couple of times."

"Yes, you brought it up the other day. About how the bell can be an interruption at a bad time. So how would it work in your school?"

"I'd get rid of the bell," Ricky said. "That way, the kids wouldn't have to move to another class until they felt ready to take on another subject. They'd know they were ready to move on when they could show the teacher they'd learned to do what the lesson they're working on asked them to do."

"Sounds good," Dad said, "but wouldn't that create chaos?"

"No. Remember? Everyone would know what they needed to practice to reach the goal of the lesson, and they'd know how to tell when they did so."

"How?"

"Like I said before, they'd find an instructor and prove to her they'd learned to do what they were supposed to learn—you know, actually demonstrate they could do it. That would be kind of like an interim assessment triggered by the student. Then they could move ahead to the next lesson. But they'd also be allowed to spend a little time fondling what they'd just learned—sort of reward themselves by basking in their new knowledge before moving on. Cool, no?"

"Sounds good to me," Dad said.

"Besides, the kids I know being home-schooled don't even have a bell. They can study and practice as long as it takes to learn what they need to know. They seem to like that arrangement a bunch."

"I'm sure they must. Any other obstacles worth talking about?"

"Sure. Textbooks."

"What's the matter with the textbooks?"

"Some of them are really boring. No examples to help the kids see how the subject has anything to do with their life, type too small to read easily, and subject matter dry as dust. It's as though some of them were written by robots locked in dungeons."

"You really are observant. Anything else?"

"Yeah. Lectures. I think I already mentioned this, too."

"Oh, come on, now. What's wrong with the lectures?"

"Nothing wrong with the *idea* of lectures, of course, but sometimes the teacher doesn't know enough about her subject to explain things well. Sometimes, the teacher gets off on her favorite hobby-horse, or tells stories that aren't relevant to the subject at hand. That wastes a lot of time the kids could use practicing what they're supposed to be learning."

Dad nodded. "Yes. I remember reading a study that must have been published fifty years ago, showing that if all the irrelevant stuff was squeezed out of a lecture session, a fifty-minute lecture wouldn't take longer than about twenty minutes."

"Wow! No kidding? Now *that's* what I'm talking about," Ricky said. "If the lecture time were streamlined, the whole course might take less time. And the practice time could be made longer. Right?"

"Absolutely," Dad said.

"Another problem with lectures is that there's little or no give and take in the rate the information comes at you. It's like being splooshed with water from a faucet that won't let you make the water gush faster, or slower, depending on how fast you could gulp it down. It comes at the same rate for everybody."

"And the problem with that is—"

"It assumes that everybody learns at the same rate. But that's crazy, because they don't, y'know. It means the information comes too fast for some and too slowly for others. If the teacher pitches her teaching to the slowest students, the rest of the class is bored and begins to get restless. Then, if their boredom causes them to act up a little, *they'll* be the ones to get punished, or doped up with something like Ritalin—"

"You know about Ritalin?" Dad said.

"Sure. All the kids know about it. It's what they do to kids who are bored and act up."

Dad decided not to follow the thread of that conversation. "Uh-huh, but I'm still not sure I understand how you would deal with the information flow problem in your own school," Dad said.

"Okay, Dad, let me try it this way. A lecturer is like a transmitter hosing all the kids down at the same time with a single stream of information. The students are the receivers of that information. But if the information hose is three inches in diameter, and the holes in the receivers'—the kids'— heads are smaller, or come in different sizes for different students, what will happen?"

"Got it. You'd get a mismatch in the rates at which the information stream can be absorbed. Some kids could take in information fast, and others would take longer to get the message."

"Yup. And the solution to this would be to replace the lectures with a coaching format," Ricky said.

"Coaching format?"

"You know, fix the rules so that when a kid needs help, he can call on the teacher for personal assistance. This would make it more likely the information transmitter—the teacher—could match her rate of information flow to what each student can handle."

"Okay, I think I've got it," Dad said.

"Good. For example, suppose you had a class with only one student. You could spend all your time making sure that one student catches on before moving to the next topic. Right?"

"So far, so good."

"Then, suppose you're given a second student, maybe not as sharp as the first one. What kind of adjustments would you have to make?"

"Got it. I'd have to divide my time between the two students who, according to your example, are not equally bright. Hmm. I'd probably find myself spending more time with the slower student and less with the brighter one."

"Right," Ricky said. "That's one way the brighter ones get short-changed on teacher attention. But what happens when you get *thirty* students, all different from one another?"

"The teaching problem is multiplied," Dad said. "You've got one transmitter, and thirty receivers who differ in learning rates, interest level, attention span, and the like."

"Exactly," Ricky said. "So that's part of what's

wrong with the lecture format. Now, if you put the lecture in the can—"

"Can?"

"You know, record it so the students can control the flow of information—make it so they're free to stop and start the information flow and work at their own pace. That would be a big step in the right direction, don'cha think?"

"Yes, I see that," Dad said. "Like reading a book where you can turn the pages at a rate that matches the speed at which you can absorb the information."

"Exactly. And you can flip back to pages you've already read if you want."

"You know," Dad said, "we do something like that in our classes at the Academy. We keep the lecture times to a minimum to make more time for practice, and we make the instructor/coaches available to sit beside a cadet who has questions and give the cadet individual guidance. That way, the trainee gets *just* the help he, or she, needs—*at the time it's needed*—and the coach doesn't have to disturb the whole class just to help one student."

"Great," Ricky said. "That's what I'm planning to do in *my* school. I'll arrange things to let students learn at their own rate. Then, when they feel they've learned the knowledge pieces, they'll be ready to practice until they think they're ready to show a teacher they can actually *do* whatever the lesson calls for them to do. If they can, they'll be signed off on that lesson and be ready to check their course map to decide which learning piece to attack next."

"I like it. But I thought you had another problem to talk about."

"I do. It's like this. When you want to find out how well your cadets can shoot, how do you do it?"

"We take them to the range and watch them shoot."

"Uh-huh. That seems pretty unwieldy, don't you think?" Ricky asked.

"Explain, please."

"Well, to do all that you have to have a range, and a range-master, and bullets and things. Right?"

"Of course. That's how it's done. You got a better idea?"

"Why not just give them a bunch of multiple-choice questions? That would be a lot cheaper and faster to do. Cheaper to grade, too."

"You can't be serious."

"Just for fun, suppose I am."

"Okay, we've talked about this before, too, but I'll play along. The only way you can find out if cadets can shoot is to watch them do it," Dad said.

"But how about if you have a cadet *observe* somebody shoot and then *tell* you what the shooter did right or wrong?"

"Nope." Dad shook his head. "That might reveal whether your cadets can *recognize* good shooting procedure when they see it, but it wouldn't tell you whether they can actually shoot."

"Okay," Ricky said, "then how about this? Instead of having the cadets *watch* a shooter, you have them write an essay on the correct way to shoot?"

"No way. You might learn if they can *talk* about shooting, but you'd *never* find out if they can actually *do* it. Look, I see where you're going with this, but the answer is still the same—the only way you can find out if a student can do what he or she is supposed to be able to do is to ask them to *do* it. Things like multiple-choice questions are mostly used as a cop-out—"

"Good one, Dad." Ricky raised a thumb and chuckled.

Dad continued. "They're sometimes useful for finding out if your students have stuffed into their heads what they need to know *before* they are ready to actually practice the main purpose of a lesson, but they're of little use for anything else."

It was Ricky's turn to say, "Explain."

"Okay, here's an example. Suppose you have a group of students being trained to dock one of those big oil tankers. There are hundreds of pieces of information that need to be learned before a student would be ready to practice docking that tanker without smashing it and killing everyone in sight."

"Wow," Ricky said.

"Exactly. You would need any number of sessions on the 'prepare-to-practice' skills. But when the object is to find out whether a student can *actually* steer a real oil tanker into a real dock, multiple-choice questions would be a worthless assessment device. Dangerous, actually."

"Dangerous how?"

"Well," Dad said, "Even if you used multiple-choice questions to find out whether they'd learned everything they needed to know before being *ready* for the docking practice, you *still* wouldn't know if they could actually dock a boat unless you watched them do it. Using multiple-choice questions might tell you if they were *prepared to practice*, but without the practice those students could still kill everyone in sight. So without seeing them *try* the docking procedure, you'll never know if they have *actually achieved* the objective of the lesson."

Ricky continued to pretend ignorance. "But multiple-choice tests are easier to use, and easier to score, aren't they?"

"So what? If they can't tell you what you really want to know, why bother? What have you gained by knowing I can *recognize* a properly-packed parachute, or can *write an essay* about the procedure for packing one? Those can be useful steps while preparing the student to practice, but if you've never seen me *do* it, you haven't learned if I've accomplished the objective of the lesson. Period. I rest my case," Dad concluded.

Ricky nodded. "Good thinking. Just to be a pest about it, what about an English course? Wouldn't multiple-choice questions be useful there?"

"Useful for what?" Dad said. "If it's a writing course, I suppose you could give students several sentences and ask them to recognize which are grammatically correct. But that wouldn't tell you whether the student could actually *write* one, would it?"

"No, I guess not," Ricky said.

"Maybe the worst thing about multiple-choice tests is they lead to phony evaluations."

"Come again?" Ricky said.

"Let's say you take a ten-item multiple-choice test on parachute-packing and get ninety percent correct answers. That ninety percent might get you an 'A,' but the item you missed could have been the item asking you how to attach the ripcord to the chute. You could get 90 percent of the questions right—with an 'A' for your effort—and still go to your doom when you jumped out of the airplane. Instead of an 'A,' your score actually should be zero."

"Hey, this is even more serious than I thought," Ricky said. "I think I'll pass a law against using multiple-choice questions in my school and—"

"Hold on a sec," Dad interrupted. "You don't want to throw out the bricks with the mortar."

"Huh?"

"Those multiple-choice questions can be a useful assessment format."

"Example?" Ricky said, echoing Dad's terse way of speaking.

"Okay, let me use an old coffee-pot example. Suppose you need your students to learn how to make a pot of coffee. Before they can practice actually *making* that coffee there are some things they need to know, like where to put the coffee, how much water to use, how to turn the pot on, and how to operate the controls. You can use multiple-choice questions to find out if students can tell you how to do those those things and are ready to practice actually making the coffee. Okay so far?"

Ricky nodded.

"But if you stopped there, all you'd know is that your students could *pick out the steps* of making a pot of coffee from a list of possibilities, and might be ready to practice making some. Here's the rub: If students got nine of the ten multiple-choice questions right, that would be ninety percent correct, so you might say that deserved an 'A,' right?"

"Right."

"So far, so good. But suppose when they actually tried *making* the pot of coffee, they did everything right—except they forgot the single step of putting the coffee into the pot. They'd *still* make ninety percent, while at the same time completely fail to make that pot of coffee. It might give them 90% on the knowing part, but a big fat *zero* on the *doing* part. Bottom line—the objective of the lesson was not accomplished because no coffee was made."

"I get it," Ricky said. "Knowing isn't the same as doing. I might use multiple-choice items to find out *why* they didn't get the coffee made, but not to find out if they actually made the coffee."

"That's why you have to be very careful about

using multiple-choice," Dad said. "They're seductive because they're so easy to use—even though they may not tell you what you need to know."

"*Dinner's ready*," Mom called from the back porch. "If you don't hurry, you'll miss out on my snarly-octopus soufflé."

"Mom sure has a cool imagination," Ricky shouted, leaping from his chair and running toward the house. "Wonder what that stuff *really* is."

Scene 6

Questions before Answers

Ricky's dad knew he was in for it as soon as he saw his son placing his chair next to his hammock. That always meant a serious man-to-man talk was imminent.

"Hi, Rick. How was school today?"

"Oh, you know ... "

"Got it. One of the girls aced you on one of your tests?"

"No, it's nothin' about girls."

"Fell asleep where no kid has slept before?"

"C'mon, Dad, be serious."

"Okay." Dad slid out of his hammock and sat cross-legged in front of his son. "Shoot."

"I got to thinking about all the neat things you showed me on the Police Academy tour the other day."

Dad knew not to interrupt while Ricky was thinking out loud.

"I saw a group of cadets being given a tour of the pistol range and they didn't even have any guns."

"Uh-huh." Failing to understand the problem, Dad said, "You find that puzzling?"

"In our school we would have to take a bunch of whole entire courses before they'd even let us *near* a range—even if we had one."

"Courses like what?"

"Oh, like the history of guns, bullet appreciation, aiming … stuff like that."

"Ah, now I get it. You're wondering why we don't teach a lot of information and sub-skills before we get to the main purpose of the course."

"Yeah, something like that. If you take them right out to the range on the first day, isn't that like giving the cadets a scalpel when they first walk into a doctoring class and telling them to take out somebody's appendix?"

"That's a good analogy, but it doesn't fit this situation," Dad said. "Showing them the range isn't the same as asking them to shoot. Actually, we *do* structure the curriculum so one idea builds on another. For example, we teach cadets how to aim a pistol *only* after teaching them how to hold their pistols safely."

"I see that, but—"

"But the very *first* thing we do is familiarize them with the range itself—in other words, we let them *experience* the ultimate purpose of that part of the course. We let them see it, feel it, and watch it in action."

"Why?"

"Because that actually *shows* them some of the

things they'll have to learn before they're ready to use the range. It faces them with some of the problems they'll have to solve before they're allowed to shoot. In other words, *it puts questions in the minds of the students* before *we begin doling out answers.*"

"Got an example, Dad?"

"Sure. Suppose you wanted to be a doctor and signed up for medical school. In the old days, that would mean you'd have to study for two whole years before you ever *saw* a patient."

"I don't follow you. What would I be doing during those two years?" Ricky asked.

"Those two years used to be called 'Basic Science,' and consisted of courses in chemistry, anatomy, physiology, pharmacology, and the like."

"So? Wouldn't I have to know about those things?"

"*Sure*, you would. In spades. But if those were the *first* things you were faced with, you wouldn't have much reason to pay attention to them. It's like this. Suppose you had to learn to drive an actual Batmobile and I began by teaching you the history of bats—"

"But why should I care about bats?"

"Exactly the point," Dad said. "If you had no idea of what you were expected to be like once you'd accomplished the learning, it would be a lot harder to tie the teaching to the real world—it would be a lot harder to motivate you to pay close attention to what I was presenting. So, if I were teaching you auto mechanics, for example, and said, 'The crankshaft is connected to the engine,' it would have a lot more meaning if you'd actually *seen* one than if you hadn't. Right?"

"I think so. You're saying it isn't only a matter of *what* has to be learned, but also the *sequence* in which it's learned."

"Precisely. If you'd never seen a golf course or watched a golfer swinging at a ball, it wouldn't make much sense to begin your instruction with the history of golf, or with the intricacies of a golf club."

"Uh-huh. I think I'm getting it now," Ricky said. "So how do the medical schools deal with that problem today? They can't just give the newbies a scalpel and ask them to practice carving out somebody's innards."

Dad chuckled. "That's an interesting image. No, the first thing they do is face the student with the kinds of situations they'll be dealing with. In other words, they show the students a patient and ask the students to describe what they see."

"I don't get it. What good would that do if the students haven't been taught anything yet?"

"It focuses their attention on what they need to learn before they can answer the questions."

"How does that work?" Ricky asked.

"A professor might gather a few students around the bed of a patient and ask them what they see. At first, they won't see much of anything, because they don't yet know what to look for."

"Ah, *now* I get it. If you begin by facing them with a problem, they'll pay more attention to what they have to learn to solve that problem."

"Exactly. Otherwise, you'll be answering questions before they've been raised in the minds of the students. That's bad pedagogy—faulty teaching practice."

"Huh?"

"Look. You're interested in soccer, aren't you?"

"You bet," Ricky said.

"Suppose you show up for soccer lessons, and even take your soccer ball to class. You're ready to play soccer, even though you don't yet know how to kick the ball. How would you feel if the instructor began with a series of lessons on the history of balls?"

"Bored to the max. Why should I care about the history of soccer balls when I'm there to learn to play the game?"

"Exactly. So, the first thing you should do is give the students actual experience with the reason for the course. If you begin by plunging them into the reason they showed up—in this case, playing soccer—and let them watch a game in action, and maybe even put them on the field to try to move the ball around—they'll be a lot more eager to learn about what you're teaching. But *right this minute*, they want to know about how to kick the ball. So that's another rule to follow in your school—if you catch someone teaching the history of a subject on the first day of a course—any course—put them right into your dungeon and feed them nothing but squiggly worms and water."

"But suppose I'm assigned to teach history? Wait, don't tell me. I think I get it. If I'm teaching a history course I should first do something to get them interested in the subject. Yeah, I happen to know the first question they'll ask is why they have to learn such a boring subject in the first place."

"Precisely," Dad said. "So ask yourself why the kids think history is boring."

"That's easy. It's because of the sequence in which the story is told. You told me that before: Just because event A *happened* before event B doesn't mean you should *teach* it in that order."

"Right. So how might you sequence a history course to excite the students' interest in the subject?"

"Oh," Ricky said, scrunching up his face in thought. "Well, to goose their interest in the subject, maybe I'd show them a short film on one of the wars. Think that would work?"

"It might, especially if you primed them with a few questions designed to pique their curiosity."

"Would that work for girls, too? I don't think they're interested in knowing about wars."

"You might be surprised at what girls are interested in. There are a lot of women in the Armed Forces, you know. In addition, thousands of women work behind the lines making, or fixing, tanks, airplanes, and munitions. The point is that you can't tell just by looking at someone what they might be interested in."

"I can see that."

"Here's an example," Dad said. "I read about

an experiment where the scientist wanted to find out what a *logical* learning sequence might look like if it were generated by a *student*."

"Really? How could he do *that?*"

"First, he rigged up a recording device to keep track of what would transpire in his sessions with his students. Then he invited several employees' wives—one at a time, of course—to his lab to be guinea pigs for the experiment. By the way, all his volunteers happened to be women because they were curious to know more about what their physicist husbands were up to during their working days. Now then, his instruction to his guinea pigs was that they would be learning something about electronics, and that he would pretend to be an infinite bag of knowledge about the subject, *but would speak only in answer to questions.* Then he shut up."

"Whoa. You serious? What happened?"

"The first thing one woman said was, 'I don't know anything about electronics.' The experimenter knew she was wrong about that, because *everyone* knows a little *something* about a lot of things, even though some of that 'knowing' may be wrong. Then the very next thing she asked about was how a TV set worked. Y'see, back then the screens on the TVs were part of a big vacuum tube inside which some of the TV components lived. She asked, 'How do you get a picture on a picture tube?'"

"Whoa," Ricky said, again. "I'll bet that threw the scientist guy for a loop."

"Yes, it sure did. But his challenge was to learn how to answer her questions in a way she would understand. But that was very difficult for the experimenter, because his head was thinking about the *other* end of the subject-matter."

"Huh?"

"He was thinking about what *he* was used to teaching first, like about electrons in orbit, and current flow, and components. Now she comes along and asks about something not usually talked about until nearer the *end* of the course. But, since the object of the experiment was to discover what *she* considered to be a logical sequence, he had to learn to turn his head around and try different ways of answering the question until she said she was ready to move on. Then, when she was finally satisfied with his answer, he shut up and waited for the next question. When he got to describing the insides of a picture tube, and said, 'Inside the picture tube there is a coil of wire,' before he could say another word, the woman said, '*Yes!* My *toaster* has a coil of wire.' She'd made a connection, you see, and it got her all revved up to learn more."

"Even though the connection she made was nuts?"

"Even so. Don't forget, the object was to find out what a logical learning sequence might look like if it were generated *by the student*. This example illustrated how the 'logical sequence' in the experimenter's head differed from what the *student* considered to be a 'logical seqence.' To wit, as soon as the experimenter said 'coil of wire,' the first thing that popped into the woman's head was that her toaster had one of those, thus making the connection."

"Wow," Ricky said. "His head must have been spinning big time."

"Yes. So you can imagine what happens when an instructor designs a course according to his *own* picture of a 'logical sequence.' The result can be a huge gap between *his* picture and *a student's* picture."

"Got it," Ricky said. "If you teach according to what *your* head tells you is a logical sequence, you might not be connecting to what the *student* thinks is a logical sequence. I think I'm beginning to get the picture."

"So you see," Dad said, "selection of the correct course content is important, but the *sequence in which that content is taught* can be just as important. I forgot to tell you that this woman got so excited by making that connection all on her own, the following day she showed up with a portable radio under her arm. She said, 'This radio doesn't work, and I'm going to fix it!' How's *that* for motivation?"

"Terrific. Did she fix it?"

"Well, when the scientist asked her what she thought might be wrong with it, after a minute or two of mental fumbling, she said she thought maybe it might be dead batteries. So the experimenter gave her some fresh batteries and showed her where to install them. When she did just that and turned the radio on, it came blaring to life. She was so thrilled she could hardly wait to show her physicist husband her accomplishment."

Ricky looked off into space as he processed what he'd just learned. "Let me see if I understand what you just said. We were talking about sequencing the instruction, but in this example *all* the sequencing was done by the student. Did I miss something?"

"Not at all," Dad said. "The message here is that if you make the objective of a lesson clear to the student, and then give the student the freedom to decide what she needs to learn to fill the gap between what she already knows, and what she needs to know in order to accomplish the objective—you may be surprised at how fast she'll do exactly that ... and beyond."

"I think I've got it," Ricky said. "If I can make the desired end result of a lesson clear and then let the *student* decide what to do to achieve that result, I may not have to do much else. Right?"

"Almost. As long as the goal is clear and you've provided the means for achieving it, you can simply stand aside until they ask for help, at which point you offer the help they asked for. Don't downplay the importance of having a readily available, and responsive, coach."

"I got it. Show 'em what they need to achieve, give them the means of getting there, and then *get out of their way.*"

"That's it," Dad said. "To the degree possible, let the students decide *how* they will accomplish the goals. That way, they will be able to avoid spending time 'learning' things they already know. And by the way, this technique works as well with men as for women."

"Boy, with that technique I won't need teachers, will I?"

Dad held up a hand and said, "Stop the train. We've missed a critical point here."

"Oh? What?"

"The point about where help will come from at the moment a student needs it."

"Oh. That's where the coaches come in, right?"

"Right," Dad confirmed. "Think about it this way. Suppose you decide to go on a trip. What means of transportation would you use?"

"Hey. How should *I* know? I don't even know where I'm supposed to be going."

"Exactly," Dad said. "If you don't know where you're going, you just might wind up someplace else."

"Of course! Got it."

"So somebody has to be able to help you point yourself in a useful direction. That's again where the coaches come in."

"I see that," Ricky said.

"Okay," Dad said. "We were talking about sequencing. Got the stomach for another example?"

"You bet."

"Once upon a time I took a correspondence course in locksmithing. I saw a little ad in a magazine that screamed, 'Be a locksmith.' Thinking that might be interesting, I signed up, mainly be-

cause I was curious about *how to pick a lock.*
Well, the instruction arrived in the form of book-
lets inside a small cardboard box, each booklet
containing three to five lessons. When I opened
the first booklet, imagine my surprise when I discovered that the *very first* lesson was on how to
pick a lock!"

"Wow! Not on the history of locks?" Ricky
asked, pretending horror.

"No, sir. I was instructed to take the combina-
tion lock out of the box and follow the instructions.
By the time I finished the lesson I was able to pick
that lock open and mail it back to the instructor as
proof of my accomplishment—proof I had learned
what I was supposed to learn."

"Cool. And you didn't even know how locks
worked and stuff, did you?"

"You got it. All I knew was that there are thousands of different kinds of lock, but at *that point* in
the learning I was far more interested in the pick-
ing than in any other part of the course. But think
about it. After that one lesson I could go around
buttonholing my friends saying, 'Hey, let me show
you how I can pick this lock.' That was hot stuff.
Think I wasn't motivated to move on to the next
lesson? I could hardly *wait* to dig in."

"So what happened next?"

"Every lesson after that taught me something
new, while at the same making me *apply* what I
had learned before. When I got to the main lesson
on lock-picking they sent me a small bag of different kinds of locks, asked me to pick and tape them

open, and mail them back to my instructor. That way, I proved to my instructor, and to myself, that I'd learned what I needed to know. That *really* made me feel good and also made me eager to dive into the next lesson. Then, sprinkled throughout the rest of the course were lessons about other intriguing subjects, such as 'Emergency entry.'"

"What's that?"

"How to get into a car or house when there isn't time to pick the lock."

"You mean burglary?"

"No. It's only burglary when a bad guy enters a premises without permission. But if a car is on fire and the driver is still in it, you'd want to know how to open that door *fast*, don't you think?"

"You bet."

"One last point. Whoever designed that course cleverly saved the so-called 'boring' stuff for last—things like how and where to buy supplies, how to organize a locksmithing business, and so on. The point is, by *then* those topics were anything *but* boring. By then I could almost smell the ink on my certificate. In other words, by the time they laid on the 'boring' stuff, I had a strong reason to pay attention to it. By then that 'boring stuff' became very important to my world."

"Wow. That's *really* cool."

"Think what would have happened if the course had started by teaching me how to buy supplies and organize a business, or had begun with the—"

"—history of locksmithing. Got it. That would

be like first teaching me how computer games got invented before letting me play one."

Dad nodded his agreement. "So, does this give you any ideas about how you'll sequence content in your own school?"

"You bet. I'll start with something about a subject the students are most interested in. Then—wait a minute—before I decide how to do *that* I'll have to know something about the students, right?"

"That would help," Dad said.

"Then, I'll have to figure out what students will be expected to do after I've finished teaching them. You know, what they'll be like when they've learned their way through the lessons."

"Yes."

"Okay, but how do I keep them motivated all the way through the course?"

"By the time you've structured your instruction according to the procedure we've just been talking about, motivation will be the least of your problems."

"It will? How come?"

"If you start out with something they're really interested in, and then sprinkle the other high-interest subjects throughout the course, you'll probably have a course that no one will want to put down—like a novel that grabs you on the first page and won't let go until you've finished the book."

"Wow," Ricky said, "so in my school every course will have to start with something the students are really interested in, even though that something might not be the most important part of the course. But ... how do I find out what they're interested in?"

"Easy. Just *ask* them. You don't have to do a scientific study, just ask a few of them what there is about the subject they might be interested in. They'll be glad to tell you, after which you'll be off and running. The trick is to start with the big picture of the subject area you're teaching, and *then* move toward the details. And, to get them interested in the importance of the subject, see if you can make the subject come alive for them."

"Gee, would that work for history, too?"

"Especially for history. To go back to your war example, suppose you invited a local war veteran to come in to your classroom and answer questions about his or her experiences? Think that would work?"

"In spades! I'll bet the kids would have a million questions."

"And I'll bet you can think of lots of other things you might do to bring any subject to life."

"*Any* subject?" Ricky asked.

"Just about. In any case, it's always worth a try to bring it to life before you jump into the subject itself."

"*Dinner*," Mom called. "*Come wash up. Monkey brains for dinner tonight.*"

"Oh boy, Dad, chicken livers in scrambled eggs! Race 'ya to the kitchen."

Scene 7

Motivation Is Not a Problem

Ricky frowned as he dragged his chair to his Dad's hammock in the back yard. He crossed his legs and sat quietly until his father let his newspaper slide to the ground.

"Hi, Rick," his Dad said. "You look troubled. Can I help?"

"I hope so. It's like this. When I put my school together I'm going to have to figure out what to do with the girls."

"I don't follow you. Can't you just put them in your dungeon?"

"C'mon, Dad, be serious. I've figured out that the school I go to was designed for girls—"

"You said something along those lines a while back. But are you serious?"

"Yes. It's pretty obvious, you know. Most of the teachers are female, and so are most of the administrators. It's pretty much like a female club."

"Is that bad?"

"Not all by itself, of course, but it ends up with

a school where the rules favor the girls. The guys should consider themselves lucky to get separate toilet facilities."

"They can't pee sitting down?"

"C'mon, Dad, get serious. We've talked about this before."

"Okay, then, remind me how the rules favor the girls?"

"It's not so much the rules ... it's just that the schools are designed for girls. Just like they're designed for right-handed kids."

"How?"

"Girls are built to sit still and be quiet, and boys are built to move around a lot—they're built to be more active. When school classrooms have rows of chairs all facing the front of the room, that arrangement kind of screams out to the teacher to lecture while the students sit and listen. That's not natural for boys. So the girls get better grades because they can pay attention longer than boys."

"And you believe that's because boys are built differently than girls?"

"Sure. What else could it be?"

"Well," Dad said, "let's think about that a bit. What do you like best about school—besides sports?"

"That's easy. Science."

"Why do you suppose that is?"

"Well, the teacher does lots of demonstrations and we get to actually do a bunch of experiments. That gives us a chance to move around and do things. I wish the science classes were longer."

"What else is there about science classes that attracts you?"

"Well, it gives us a chance to get our hands on it."

"I see. And what do you wish was shorter?"

"English ... social studies ... history ... you know, the boring stuff."

"Can you tell me why those subjects are boring?"

"That's easy. We just sit there and listen to the teacher talk about things we're not interested in. It only gets kind of interesting when she stops talking and we get to *do* something—"

"Like what, for instance?"

"Like spelling practice, and spelling bees. And like when we get to draw maps of the history things we study."

"So what does that tell you?"

"Uh ... wait, I think I get it. Things get interesting when we get to *do* something ... something besides just sit quietly and listen."

"So far, so good," Dad said. "But aren't there times when your eyes and ears are glued to your teacher during those 'talk about' times?"

Ricky scratched his head. "Yeah, I suppose. When coach talks to us about the next game coming up and he's teaching us the plays we're going to use."

"You pay attention to every word, right?"

"You bet. If we don't, we're likely to get killed by the other team."

"Aha! So you're saying that you pay close attention when there is a *reason* to do so."

"Uh-huh."

"Even if you're a *boy?*"

"What do you—oh, I get it. If the stuff is interesting, the boys can pay attention as well as the girls. That it?"

"Part of it."

"What part did I miss?"

"The part about what *makes* something interesting."

"Well, I just told you. It gets interesting when it has something to do with what we *need to know* before we can actually *do* something—like, we have to know the plays before coach lets us onto the field."

"Got another example?" Dad asked.

Ricky squeezed his eyes shut in thought. "Okay, here's one: Remember the time you took a bunch of us to the county morgue on a private field trip? We were pretty grossed out about the idea, until you told us about all the cool things we were going to see. Then we could hardly wait to see the inside of the place. Y'know, I'd never thought about where bodies go when they get dead."

Dad snorted at Ricky's choice of an example. "I suppose that qualifies."

"Well, it got me curious about how the world works and stuff, like how water comes out of our faucets when we turn the handle. So I'm looking things up on the web."

"In other words, you're self-schooling because you have questions you want answers to."

"I guess. Wait, I think I got it. I've been struggling with how I was going to make my school work with both boys and girls. But I won't have to worry about their being different if I can find a way to give them a *reason* to learn the stuff. You know, a reason that has meaning to *them*."

"Exactly. But let me ask you something, Rick. Even though there is a difference between boys and girls in their ability to sit still, do you think the girls are *happy* about sitting still? Don't you think *they* would be more interested in the topic if they were allowed to get their hands into it ... and to move around some while getting the actual feel of the subject?"

"Well, yeah ... I suppose so. Now that you mention it, I think you're right. The girls are sure active when they're playing basketball, or volleyball and stuff. It's only when they get into the classroom that things can get boring. But if I can get both the boys and the girls doing something other than sitting and listening, the difference between them should go away. Right?"

"Yes," Dad said. "Actually, there are many ways to motivate students. Would you like to hear about one you'll never hear from anyone else?"

"You mean a secret way?"

"Not for a minute. This technique has been available to everyone for a long time. So let me ask you: When you were in second grade, say, was it difficult for the teacher to get the attention of the kids?"

"Ha. You bet. Instead of listening to the

teacher, all they wanted to do was run and scream."

"Exactly," Dad said.

"What do you mean?" Ricky seemed confused by Dad's single-word reply.

"It's like this. Suppose you could turn the urge to 'run and scream' into a way of motivating students to pay attention?"

"I don't get what you're saying."

"Let me tell you a true story. I learned about this while reading some psychological research literature on motivation. A research scientist named Dr. Lloyd Homme did some fascinating experiments. He had a class of kids in the early grades, and when he tried to focus their attention on what he was trying to teach them, all they wanted to do was run and scream. Sound familiar?"

"Uh huh."

"One day he discovered a way to turn that urge to run and scream into a reward for good behavior."

"I don't get it," Ricky said.

"When he got the attention of the class for a few seconds he said, 'If you will pay close attention to what I'm about to tell you for *three minutes*, then we'll *all* go run and scream.'"

"Wow. Now I get it. He used running and screaming as a reward for paying attention. Right?"

"Absolutely correct. When the three minutes were up, Dr. Homme gave the signal and everybody got up to run and scream ... and laugh and giggle—and get their blood flowing. Then, when that time limit was up, the kids all sat down quietly to find out what would happen next."

"Well, what *did* happen next?"

"The kids were then told, 'If you'll pay attention for *five minutes*, we'll all go run and scream.' And they did."

"Did you say this was a *true* story?"

"Absolutely. And it wasn't long before the kids would sit for longer and longer periods of time, because the reward for doing so was so delightful. The kids never realized that all that running and screaming and laughing was also healthy."

"I could never get away with that in *my* school," Ricky said.

"Well," Dad said, "you'll never know unless you try. If it's *your* school, you'll be able to try pretty much anything you want. By the way, during all that running and screaming, Dr. Homme discovered he had an even stronger reward at his fingertips."

"What?"

"He discovered that the thing the kids would work hardest for was the 'reward' of sitting him in his swivel chair, spinning him 'round and 'round, and pushing him around the classroom floor."

"You serious? Boy, that must have been a hoot."

"And don't forget, 'rewards' like these were—and still are—all available to anybody, and they were all *free*."

"Like I said, Dad, I could *never* do that in my

own school."

"Why not?"

"Uh, I think the teachers would laugh at me. It's pretty radical, you know."

"But when they see the results ..."

"Uh ... I guess you're right about that."

"So," Dad said, "you could try, and you could think about other things you might do to get the same results."

"But how would I find out what kinds of things I could use as free rewards? Wait, don't tell me. Uh, I could watch what the kids do and what they talk about. And, I suppose I might come right out and ask them. Right?"

"Yup, I think you've got it," Dad said. "While we're on the subject, can you stand another example of how easy it is to motivate students?"

"Sure," Ricky said. "Pour it on me."

"Okay. I remember visiting a course for 'problem' kids who were just entering their teenage years. They were sort of the troublemakers of the school."

"They must have been bored silly. So what happened?"

"The instructors set up a room with tables lined up along three walls. Then they placed a sequence of tasks on the tables, along with a sign on the wall above each task. The first sign said, 'If you can do *this*, you'll be worth fifty cents an hour.' An arrow pointed down toward the task. The next task in line was a little more complicated. The sign said, 'If you can do *this*, you'll be worth seventy-five cents an hour.'"

"I get it, I get it," Ricky said, leaping from his chair. "I get it. The students could actually *see* the results of learning the tasks. They could smell the value *to them* of learning them. Right?"

"Right. They could actually *see* how learning to do the tasks could make their lives better."

"Did it work?" Ricky asked.

"Like you wouldn't believe. Those kids worked their tails off to master those tasks. And, there was a secret bonus."

"Secret? What secret?"

"Sometimes they had to learn to read a little something before they could perform the task. For others, they had to learn to do a little math."

"Sneaky!"

"I suppose you could look at it that way. Actually, what happened was that the process gave them a *reason*—a real need—to learn some of what is often thought of as boring subjects."

"Wow! What a great idea!"

"And while they were learning, they had to move around, which also helped solve the so-called motivation problem."

"That's really great," Ricky said. "That means they could find out how much they're worth even while they're learning."

"Yes," Dad said. "And knowing something about how much you're worth is something almost everyone cares about. But I've got an even better example. This one'll blow your mind," Dad said, smiling.

"I can hardly wait."

"It's like this. There were these four teachers, y'see, teaching in a school where kids were so bored they only came to school one or two days a week."

"Sounds like push-outs."

"You got it. Well, one day those teachers got together and announced to the kids—these were high school kids—'We're going to throw out this boring curriculum.'"

"Boy, I'll bet that got their attention."

"Big time. Then the teachers dropped the bomb. They said, 'Instead, we're going to teach you all how to *fly!*' By then the kids' eyes and ears were glued to the teachers, wondering what was coming next."

"So what happened?"

"When the course began, the very *first* thing the teachers did was send those kids—three at a time—up for a short flight in a real four-seat airplane."

"Wow! How did they manage to do that?"

"The local commercial aviation folks heard about the project and were eager to help. They provided the teachers with all sorts of equipment, maps, and even lent them the airplanes the kids got to fly—with a certified pilot on board, of course."

"Hey, sign ... me ... up!"

"And then each kid was given five or ten minutes in the pilot's seat so they could actually steer the plane."

"Way cool," Ricky said. "That must have been the biggest whoop of their lives."

"Absolutely. Not only that, when they landed, they became instant heroes in their neighborhood. After that, they could hardly *wait* to see what was coming next."

"Wait a minute, Dad. Something smells fishy here. How could they fly an airplane if all they knew how to do was steer it?"

Dad grinned. "I think you already know. Obviously, they couldn't. There's a big difference between just steering and keeping an airplane level, and actually *flying* that plane. But those few minutes of steering the plane were a huge thrill for them, and they desperately wanted more. Now then, to *stay* in the flight course, the kids had to learn how to read maps and manuals, how to calculate fuel loads, and how to speak clear English, and a lot more."

"English? Why?"

"English is the world-wide language of flying, so no matter where in the world you fly, you have to be able to understand the voice from the tower, and speak clear enough English to make it easy for the tower operators to understand *you*."

"Gee. So what happened after that?"

"The teachers emptied the classroom of all the desks and chairs, and with more help from local aviation—"

"Help?"

"Uh-huh. Like I said, the local aviation folks donated engines, parts, tools, manuals, maps. It gave them a big kick out of being able to contribute to the experiment. As for the kids, they could hardly wait to get to school in the morning to start working on their projects. Within minutes they were all totally involved. When I walked into that room one day, nobody even bothered to look up. They were all on their hands and knees totally engrossed—taking an engine apart, putting it back together, practicing their map-reading, even making a wind tunnel, and helping each other succeed. It was wonderful to see."

"No lectures?"

"No lectures. But ... lots and lots of individual and small-group coaching. And it wasn't until later that the kids began to realize they were learning all those 'boring' subjects they disliked so much."

"You mean like reading, and speaking clearly, and measuring, and things?"

"Right on."

"So how did it work out?"

"The absentee rate and the push-out rates went way down and the kids' grades in *all* their subjects went up that year. See what I meant when I said you wouldn't have to worry about the alleged 'motivation problem'?"

"Yeah. Then what happened?"

"Well, son, that's the sad part of the story. The program was cancelled."

"Cancelled? But why?"

"I don't really know. There could be many reasons, but cancelled it was. If you ask me, I think some of the other faculty were envious of the success of those four teachers."

"Aww, Dad, you just made this whole thing up, right?"

"Not for a minute. I can let you read the published reports if you'd like. It's a true story. Unfortunately, it's a story that's been repeated many times in many places. Why, I remember the time—"

"*Dinner*," Mom called from the back porch, swinging a dish towel over her head. "*Bloody moo-pies for dinner, so hurry up!*"

"Oh boy," Ricky said, climbing out of his chair. "Hamburgers and ketchup. Race ya to the table!"

Scene 8

The Functional Citizen

When Dad headed for his late afternoon break, he found Ricky already seated patiently in his chair. Today, the boy had his iPad in his hand, so Dad knew a really *serious* conversation was on the agenda.

"Hi, Rick. How was school?"

"Hi, Dad. School was so-so, but I had trouble paying attention to the teacher."

"Why? Dreaming about tonight's game?"

"Come on, Dad."

"Okay. So what gives?"

"Well," Ricky said, "I couldn't stop thinking about what we talked about yesterday. You know, about the teachers who took the kids up in an airplane before they taught them anything about the history of wings, and stuff."

"And that troubled you because ...?"

"Oh no, not troubled. I just got to thinking about how the same technique could be used in other subject areas. Could it?"

"Sure thing. As a matter of fact, it's already been done in any number of places and in a variety of subject areas."

"No kidding?"

"Absolutely not. For example, instead of teaching kids how to fly airplanes, you could use the techniques to teach them how to be almost anything you could mention—pilots, chefs, cops, teachers, scientists—even motion picture directors."

"You could? How would that work?"

"Well, let's think about it. What goes into making a film?"

"Gee, I dunno."

"Sure, you do. Suppose you were asked to direct a movie. At the very least, you'd need a camera—"

"Oh, I get it. I'd need actors, and a script, a sound engineer, sound effects guys, and make-up people, at least."

"Right. Now for a stupid question. Why would you need a script?" Dad prompted.

"So the actors will know what to say?"

"Of course. And to do that, the actors would have to know how to—"

"*Read.* Got it. And they'd have to know how to speak clearly, too."

"Absolutely. What else would you need?"

Ricky scrunched his forehead in thought. "Well ... they'd need to be able to measure the distance from the camera lens to the actors—"

"Which means they'd have to be able to—"

"Use a measuring instrument of some sort. Right?"

"You bet," Dad said. "Do you see that you've just described some of the elements that make up that 'boring' curriculum the kids talk about?"

"Yeah. But it wouldn't be boring any more because the kids would be learning things they needed to know before they could get at the fun stuff—the stuff they *wanted* to do."

"I suppose you could put it that way," Dad said. "But can you imagine the fun the kids would have if the teacher had them practice reading movie scripts to each other in front of the class? Maybe even have them writing scripts."

"Hey, I'll bet that would be a real blast. The kids could practice their reading and their writing, and even practice speaking clearly, all in one shot. This is fun, Dad. Can we try a harder one?" Ricky squiggled closer to the edge of his chair.

"Sure thing."

"Suppose," Ricky said, "you wanted to teach somebody to be a detective? What would you do first?"

"Easy," Dad said. "First, I'd introduce them to some real live detectives and ask them to tell you a few war stories about their exciting cases—"

Ricky whipped his hands over his ears to feign alarm. "What? You wouldn't begin with the history of detecting?" Ricky said.

"Good man. I think you're getting wise to this teaching game. Now then, after giving them some perspective on what detectives *do*, I'd show them a table full of the equipment they might have to learn to use—like weapons, disguise kits, listening devices, handcuffs, report forms, traffic tickets, and so on. Stuff like that."

"Boy, that'd be great. What then?"

"I'd take them to look into one of the interrogation rooms, and along the way let them see detectives sitting at their desks typing up their case reports. Think that might pique their curiosity?"

"You bet. Mine, too."

"By then you'd be able to get the trainees thinking about what skills they would need, and about what they'd have to know before practicing those skills."

"Like what?"

"Well, before they could practice typing reports, they'd have to be able to—?"

"Read, right?"

Dad nodded. "You got it. What else?"

"Uh ... use a keyboard?"

"Absolutely. Wouldn't make much difference whether they used one finger or twelve; they'd just have to know where the keys are and what to do with them. Here's another example. Before we let our cadets actually practice shooting, we make sure they know when, and when not, to shoot. That takes a lot more learning and practice than just learning to pull a trigger."

"It does?"

"Absolutely. Any idiot can pull a trigger, but it takes a lot of learning to know when *not* to shoot. Can you guess some of the things they'd have to know?"

"Uh ... well ... how to aim?"

"What else?"

"Uh, the laws of shooting?"

"Good. And to learn the laws of shooting it would be useful to know how to—?"

"Read."

"Right on. And you can actually practice learning to recognize the difference between 'shoot' situations and 'don't shoot' situations without even using a gun."

"You can? How?"

"One way would be to show the trainees video-recorded scenes of shooting situations, then stop the video at the crucial point and ask them to holler out, *'Shoot,'* or, *'No Shoot.'* That gives them actual practice in recognizing when and when *not* to squeeze the trigger—all without hurting somebody by accident. And once they've learned *that* skill, they'll be safe around all kinds of weapons."

"Cool."

"So, if you keep asking what students would have to be able to do before they were ready to practice the object of that particular lesson, you'd have a list of skills and knowledge *any* detective would have to have in order to earn a badge ... and that list would look—in part—very much like what you think of as that 'boring old school curriculum.' And that, m'boy, is how you derive a curriculum that is relevant to accomplishing your important learning objectives."

"I see that," Ricky said. "Y'know, Dad, I'm beginning to think this school thing is a lot easier than it looks."

Dad suppressed a chuckle. "How so?"

"Easy. All I have to do is figure out what the kids need to be able to do before I let 'em graduate, and then work backward to the things they'd have to learn before they could actually practice those things."

"Good man."

"That way," Ricky said, "they could see the *reason* to learn each of those things. Bet that would really *clobber* the push-out rate, don'cha think?"

"It certainly should help. You really *are* smarter than the average bear."

"Can we try another example?"

"Okay, pick one."

Ricky thought for a few moments. "I've got one. What would I have to know if I wanted to write some software for my computer?"

"Okay, you tell me," Dad said.

"Oh. Well, for one thing, I'd have to be able to read what's on the computer screen ... and how to use the keyboard."

"Go on."

"I'd have to be able to write instructions in machine language."

"Yes. What if your computer crashes?"

"What? Oh, I get it. I'd have to be able to read the troubleshooting manual—if there is one. Maybe I'd have to be able to use a phone—you know, speak clearly and all that—to call Tech Support ...

and it wouldn't hurt to know how to solve common troubles so I could fix my own problems." Ricky's grin told Dad he was enjoying the conversation.

"Right. There's more, of course, but you've got the hang of it."

"Yeah. I'm beginning to see the pattern. Before I can do just about anything more advanced than coloring between the lines with crayons, I'd have to be able to read, write, and know how to do something in the way of math ... and speak clearly enough to be understood. And the way to teach those things is to make those topics interesting by wrapping them around a subject the students are curious about."

"I think you're almost ready to take charge of that school you're salivating for. If you'd like, I could tell you about an interesting study where the principles we've been talking about were applied to an entire school curriculum."

"Really? Lay it on me."

"I learned about this one when I was still teaching high school. Y'see, there were a couple of scientists who worked for a research company in California a few decades ago. Their task was to lay out a revised curriculum for grades one through twelve."

"Wow! Sounds like a big job."

"Totally."

"So what did they do?"

"First, they defined what they called 'The Functional Citizen.'"

"Huh?"

"They described what a person would have to know and be able to do to qualify for graduation from high school—in other words, to be qualified to be let loose into the community."

"Is that possible?" Ricky asked.

"Sure. They began by describing the consumers of the high school graduate."

"Consumers? Explain, please."

"Okay," Dad said. "What happens after graduation? Where do those high-school graduates go?"

"They go get a job."

"Good. What else?"

"Oh, they might go to college—"

"Or maybe join the military?" Dad added.

"Okay, I get it. They might go into the church business, or even to jail. They might even want to get married. Hey, this is really fun."

Dad smiled. "Then what do you suppose the scientists did next?"

"That's easy. Once they knew what the end result should look like, they could play, 'What would someone have to be able to do before ...'"

"Right. Once they had that list of skills, they could keep working down the ladder until they got to the bottom—"

"Which was reading, and writing, and speaking, and mathematizing—"

"Mathematizing?" Dad looked puzzled.

"I just made that up," Ricky said, grinning.

"Uh-huh. Don't forget research."

"Oh yeah, I forgot. They'd have to be able to locate whatever information they needed to solve whatever problem they were facing."

"Right," Dad said. "And once they had this pile of skills on the table like a bunch of jig-saw pieces, they could begin to put them into some kind of order."

"How did they—wait a minute—I think I've got it. They played, 'before someone could learn to do this they would have to learn to do that'... and built some kind of map so students could see at a glance which lessons they were qualified to attack next."

"You really *are* sharp."

"Did it work?"

"Sure, it did," Dad said. "But it didn't last, because once they built a curriculum in that manner, they discovered they didn't need twelve years of public schooling to make a Functional Citizen."

"Is that a true story?"

"Sure is. The scientists discovered that if you eliminated most of the repetition usually found in the typical K-12 curriculum, you could make Functional Citizens in around six years."

"No kidding?"

"Nope. But that isn't likely to happen."

"Why not, Dad?"

"Because during their younger years, students' brains aren't mature enough to appreciate and understand some of the skills they would be expected to learn."

"Like what, for example?"

"Well ... like manners—"

"Hey, I got manners. I always say 'please' and

'thank you,' and I don't eat with my elbows on the table, neither. Do I?"

"No, you don't, and that's a really good start."

"So what else is there?" Ricky asked.

Dad's head scrambled for an example his son might understand. "Well, think about it this way. You're a ten-year-old who has learned all sorts of math, right?"

"Sure thing."

"And you even know a lot about physics and chemistry."

"You bet."

"But you're not yet old enough to appreciate the importance of girls."

"Yikes! Are you serious?"

"Absolutely. For example, at this stage of your life, you don't see a need to learn the kind of manners that will keep you alive when you do discover them. There's nothing wrong with *you*; it's just that your brain hasn't grown enough to grasp that concept."

"What concept?"

"Girls. Good manners. And a few other things. Haven't you noticed that the older guys bust their buns to attract the attention of the girls?"

"Yeah. I can't figure out what they see in them."

"My point exactly. That's only because some of your body parts haven't grown to the point where they've kicked in. So not only does the curriculum have to be taught in an efficient way, the various topics need to be presented at an age where the students minds and bodies are ready to deal with them."

"I see what you mean," Ricky said. "And I think there's something else I'll need to do to make the Functional Citizen idea work."

"Oh?" Dad said. "What might that be?"

"Well, back when you were a kid, all it took to make a Functional Citizen out of you was teach you how to work a plow, milk a cow, drive a tractor, and buy supplies at the feed store. That's in addition to reading and writing, and so on."

"Whoa," Dad said. "Just how *old* do you think I am?"

"Just kidding, Dad," Ricky said. "I was just trying to make the point that the world keeps changing and I'll have to keep changing my curriculum to keep up. Nowadays, the Functional Citizen curriculum would have to include things that didn't even exist back then."

"Like what?"

"Well," Ricky said, "things like driving a computer, and using the Internet, and sending emails, and how to use the latest version of what used to be the dial telephone, and a bunch of other things that didn't exist when you were a kid."

"And what does that tell you?"

Ricky thought for a minute before answering. "It tells me I'll have to keep updating my curriculum to keep up with new things. I'll have to keep on adding new skills that will have to be taught if I'm to make Functional Citizens."

"And," Dad added, "maybe deleting obsolete skills, like how to use buggy whips?"

"Yeah. That, too."

"But what about skills like problem-solving and the like? To be successful in a changing world, Functional Citizens will need to be able to handle the challenges of the times, won't they?"

"Sure," Ricky said, "and I'll have to work those into my curriculum as well. Even so, I still wouldn't need twelve years to do the job. Uh ... what do you think I could I do with the time we save?"

"Well, you could let the students spend more time *practicing* their skills, so those skills would stick beyond just the current class or school term. And you could include more field trips to give students actual hands-on experience with the real world. And ... uh ... might that be a good time to think about reducing the amount of homework assignments?"

"Wow! Now *that's* a great idea. That would be a big hit for sure. I bet the parents would like it, too."

"Why?"

"Well, come on, Dad. They wouldn't have to spend so much time helping with homework." Ricky frowned in thought. "But if these ideas work like you say, how come they're not used in the schools?"

"Ahh, I'm afraid the answer to that question involves the dreary subject of politics."

"Politics?"

"Yup. That's where the strongest pressures *against* improving the schools—where the *really* big obstacles to maximizing student capabilities— are hiding. But that's a story for another time—"

"*Dinner*," Mom called from the back porch. "Weeds and bunny droppings for dinner. Come wash up."

"Wow, Dad, baked beans and salad. Let's go."

"Not so fast, boy-o. Salad and beans means it's *my* turn to cook."

"Oh ... uh ... well ... in that case, maybe we ought to settle for pizza. I'll go call it in."

Scene 9

Listening — A Magic Key

Ricky leaped up the front steps of his house, dropped his book bag onto the kitchen floor on his way out the back door, hopped over the three back steps leading to the yard, and sprinted toward the two palm trees holding the family hammock. His Dad was already reading the daily newspaper, so Ricky hurried to settle himself into his chair.

"Sorry I'm late, Dad. For some reason, they let us out early, so I got to spend a little extra time with one of my three tutees and forgot about the time. And I wanted to ask you about something."

"Okay, but wait a minute. Did you say 'three tutees'?"

"You know, tutors tutor the tutees."

"Got it," Dad said. "But *three* tutees? Last I heard, you were only coaching *one* student."

"Yeah," Ricky said. "I guess word is getting around, 'cause they're beginning to line up for help."

"Line up? You mean figuratively, right?"

"Uh-huh. And you know what?"

"What?" Dad said.

"One of my tutees is a *girl*."

"Really? Tell me about her."

"Well, she's a girl—"

"Yes, I got that. What about it?"

"It's kinda strange."

"Strange how?" Dad asked.

"Uh, she came to me about three weeks ago, and asked for my help with some math problems."

"What's so strange about that?"

"It turned out she doesn't need *any* help with math," Ricky said. "She's so smart, she zips through the assignments like a snake through tall grass."

Dad thought for a few moments before asking, "So, what are you doing about it?"

"Well, at first I really didn't know what to do, or what to say. She was kinda shy and looked at her lap a lot, so there was a lot of silence."

"So?"

"So when I didn't say anything right away, she finally started talking. After she kept on talking for a while, she looked up at me, and even smiled a little."

"Then what?" Dad prodded.

"She started telling me about her brothers. She's got five older brothers."

"And," Dad said, "I'll bet they're no help to their little sister."

"Worse than that, Dad. All her brothers are into sports, and her dad coaches one of the high school football teams."

"Ouch."

"Yeah, they give Lila a hard time about being smart."

"What about her parents?" Dad asked. "Don't *they* give Lila any encouragement for being smart?"

"I don't think so," Ricky said. "Every time there's a game night, her Mom is there to cheer her guys on while her Dad runs up and down the side-lines, coaching. They take Lila to the games, but she doesn't like sports. She'd *much* rather stay home with the dog and read."

"How are you handling the situation?" Dad asked.

"Well, for one thing, I keep telling her there's nothing wrong with being smart. I tell her she should be proud of her smarts because they let her do things that less smart people can't do. She seems to perk up at that. You know, Dad, we've only had three sessions together, but she already seems like a different person."

"How different?"

"Well, she smiles more, and she even looks at me more. She's starting to be a lot of fun."

Dad thought for a few moments, then said, "I'd say you're doing her more good than you'll ever imagine. Keep it up."

"But," Ricky said, "I'm not doing any *work*. Mainly, I'm just listening to her."

"Believe it or not, *listening* is the key to your success. I think you're learning the secret of improving someone's self-esteem."

Ricky thought for a few moments. "I'm going to have to rattle that idea around some. I'll look it up."

"Try looking up 'self-confidence.' By the way," Dad said, "does your teacher know about your new hobby?"

"Sure. A couple times I had to ask her for help in explaining a math concept to one of my guys. She was very helpful. She listened to how I tried explaining the problem to the student, and when I finished, she said she would make notes on how I handled the issue, so she could explain it better next time it came up in her class."

"Sounds like you're even teaching your teacher. That's great! You deserve a lot of credit for taking this on."

"Thanks, Dad, but *I'm* learning from it, too. I think I'm getting better at explaining things as we go along."

"I'm sure that's true." Changing the subject, Dad said, "Didn't you tell me there was something you wanted to ask about?"

"Yes, sir. Do you know what 'social promotion' means?"

"Unfortunately, I do. 'Social promotion' is the polite term for the process of passing a failing student on to the next grade. How did you happen to hear about it?"

"I heard a couple of teachers talking about it in the lunch room. But did I hear you right? Is there *really* such a thing?" Ricky said.

"Yes indeed, and it's a deplorable practice."

"Why would anybody *do* that, Dad? Isn't it dishonest to send students to the next grade before they've learned what they were supposed to learn in *this* grade? If you ask me, I think it's unfair to the students. It means they're being dumped into a class they're not ready for."

"Yes, it *is* unfair to the student," Dad said. "The school is definitely short-changing students when they promote them before they're ready."

"So why *do* they do it?"

"Well," Dad said, "I think it's because the teachers are *afraid* to hold students back when they're not ready for promotion, because some parents get pretty angry when their kid is held back. Besides, the student probably knows he's not ready for the promotion, but *really* resents having to think of himself as a failure. On the other hand, the big problem with holding a kid *back* when he's not ready for promotion can be just as bad."

"How so?" Ricky asked.

"Not only are such kids bored by having to sit through all the stuff they've already been through, they feel stigmatized at having to do it with kids who are younger, and frustrated at seeing their old friends move on. If they didn't *already* dislike school, this would be a good way to create, and cement, that dislike into place. It's a problem that won't be solved as long as the school is on the 'grade' system."

"Well, that couldn't happen in *my* school,"

Ricky said.

"Oh? Why not?"

"I think I already told you. I won't *have* grades. In *my* school the students will be expected to practice until they learn what they're supposed to learn. If they can't do it the first or second time, they'll just practice some more. They won't have to worry about passing or flunking, because my system will be designed to let the students practice until they get it."

"Good plan. But I think we both know you'll have some students along the way who will *never* get it—at least not within the teaching time you'll have. What might you do when that happens?"

"Uh ... I guess I'll just have to look for someone actually qualified to teach that type of student."

"You know," Dad said, "'social promotion' is also a pretty popular way of getting rid of *workers* who aren't working up to expectation."

"It is? How do they do *that*?"

"Well," Dad said, "in the business world, for instance, they either transfer them to somebody else's department, or just promote them to a higher level. It's a popular way of getting rid of people who, for whatever reason, are a thorn in somebody's side. They don't *call* it 'social promotion,' but that's pretty much what it is."

"Bummer," Ricky said.

"In any case, the practice is pretty widespread. Not only do schools promote unqualified students, some school administrators keep unqualified teachers as well."

"Why?"

"Because the laws make it almost impossible to fire an incompetent teacher."

"Well, Dad, *my* school will be on the 'up-and-up,' as they say."

"I'm sure you'll be able to make your system work just fine."

Ricky looked off into the distance while forming a thought. "Dad, I have a question."

"Shoot."

"Do you think I'll *ever* get my own school?"

Dad smiled. "Hey, didn't you just tell me you already have three 'tutees' on your string?"

"Yup. Three so far."

"Well, it seems to me you've *already* got your own school going. To be called a 'school,' an educational enterprise doesn't have to be plunked into a little brick school-house, you know."

"What?" Ricky pounced on the idea. "Gosh, you're right! I never thought about it that way." His head began running with the implications of this stupendous insight. "Now that you mention it, I guess you could say that all the home-schooling people have their own schools, whether or not those 'schools' have their own separate buildings."

"That's true," Dad said.

"Wow! That is way cool." Ricky's brain was bubbling with ideas. He felt as though a new door to the future had just opened.

"So if I've *already* got my own school, that means I won't need the loan and you can keep your million dollars—"

"Gee, thanks a lot," Dad said.

"You can keep the bucks in a safe place until I need a building and things. Gosh," Ricky continued, words tumbling from his mouth, "when I get my driver's license, you'll be able to buy me a car, or maybe a van, and I can drive my school around to wherever my tutees happen to be ... that would be really useful if I'm tutoring someone who happens to be disabled."

"I can see your brain is flying in all directions, mapping out a plan."

"I'll have to change it as I go along, though, but I'm pretty jazzed about this as it is."

"I can tell, and I'm delighted to see it. And don't forget, you've got even more going for you."

"I do?"

"You're already getting a lot of coaching experience as you work with your tutees. Seems to me you'll be off to a roaring start by the time you're ready to add a building or three to your traveling school."

"Yeah," Ricky said, his eyes still twinkling with excitement.

"So are your tutees progressing?"

"Pretty well. Seems like mostly all I have to do is listen to them explain the problem they're having, then ask them a few questions to help them work it out for themselves."

"Does that work?"

"Sure seems to. They get all excited when they discover they can solve some of their own problems. Then they come back for more."

"So what's your next move?"

Ricky thought in silence as his brain processed the question. "I think I'll have to hunker down and learn everything about everything. I'll start with the subjects I'm taking now, and then branch out to the ones they teach in the higher grades."

"Uh-huh. But don't forget that there are resources at your fingertips that can solve many of your problems with a few keystrokes."

"I don't get you," Ricky said.

"Sure you do! You've been using those resources to teach yourself. If you have questions without answers, you can ask Google any question you'd like, and one or more answers will come flying back to you. For example, you could ask it, 'How do I explain Boyle's Law to a fifth grader?' Or, 'How can I teach the concept of fractals?' Ask it anything. The answers may amaze you. Google is a resource everybody should know about. And it's certainly not the *only* source."

"Gee, you're right, Dad. I don't know why I didn't think of it that way before now. It's a wonderful resource ... and there are others like it." Ricky thought for a few moments, then added, "Uh, is this a good time for me to ask if I could have a more powerful computer ... please? With more memory and a bigger screen, maybe?"

"Well, since I'm no longer on the hook for a million non-existent bucks, I think it might be arranged," Dad said, smiling.

And so it came to pass.

Useful Resources

Books

How to Turn Learners On ... Without Turning Them Off. Robert F. Mager, Mager Associates, Inc., Revised Third Edition, 2012.

Measuring Instructional Results. Robert F. Mager, Mager Associates, Inc., Revised Third Edition, 2012.

Analyzing Performance Problems. Robert F. Mager, Mager Associates, Inc., Revised Third Edition, 2012.

Goal Analysis. Robert F. Mager, Mager Associates, Inc., Revised Third Edition, 2012.

Websites

Homeschool World: *www.home-school.com*

Waldorf Schools: *www.whywaldorfworks.com*

Montessori Schools: *www.montessori.edu*

Khan Academy: *www.khanacademy.com*

Wizards Behind the Scenes

An old saying has it that "the proof of the pudding is in the eating." Well, the proof of a manuscript is in the tryouts. Unless a manuscript is bumped up against some of those for whom it is specifically intended, the writer will never know how well his work accomplished its mission.

So bump I did. And bump back *they* did!

But wait! Just who *are* these people who poked and prodded my hard-earned words, tsked at my favorite non-sequiturs, and snickered at my convoluted sentences? Who indeed!

Actually, they are knowledgeable people residing all the way from Hawaii to Maine, and points in between. They are welcome "volunteers" who offered to read one or another early draft—or portions thereof—and helped unscramble my garbled utterings into an edit-ready product.

What? You want *names?* Well, I should think so. After all, they deserve to be exposed, so here they are. Perhaps you should stand in awe as you read ...

David Cram, Margaret Stewart, Rodney L. Cron, Shuk Fon Yuen, Peter Pipe, Richard Ham, Bonnie Abney, Dick Stewart, Linda Amato, Dan Raymond, Chrissy Dart, Gabriel Mager, Libby Muelhaupt, BJ Southwick, and Amber Southwick.

There! Each and every one deserves my deepest gratitude for the time and wisdom they offered. But there's more.

Eileen W. Mager performed the delicate editorial surgery (more than thrice) on what I mistakenly considered to be a polished draft; cutting, pasting, and tsking as she shook her head at my barely misspelled words.

Tony Amato, of Amato Image Design, created the cover out of thin air and buckets of talent.

To all, I bow deeply with thanks for their efforts on my behalf.

Of course, errors and omissions are attributed to my fractious computer, *Glitch*.

Robert F. Mager
Carefree, Arizona